PURE
EYES,
CLEAN
HEART

A Couple's Journey to Freedom from Pornography

JEN FERGUSON *and*
CRAIG FERGUSON

DISCOVERY HOUSE
P U B L I S H E R S®

Feeding the Soul with the Word of God

Pure Eyes, Clean Heart: A Couple's Journey to Freedom from Pornography

© 2014 Craig and Jen Ferguson

Discovery House is affiliated with RBC Ministries, Grand Rapids, Michigan.

Requests for permission to quote from this book should be directed to: Permissions Department, Discovery House Publishers, P.O. Box 3566, Grand Rapids, MI 49501, or contact us by e-mail at permissionsdept@dhp.org

Unless otherwise indicated, all Scripture quotations are taken from the *Holy Bible,* New Living Translation, copyright © 1996, 2004, 2007, 2013 by Tyndale House Foundation. Used by permission of Tyndale House Publishers, Inc., Carol Stream, Illinois 60188. All rights reserved.

Scripture quotations marked NASB are from the New American Standard Bible®, copyright © 1960, 1962, 1963, 1968, 1971, 1972, 1973, 1975, 1977, 1995 by The Lockman Foundation. Used by permission. (www.Lockman.org)

ISBN: 978-1-62707-056-0

Interior designed by Melissa Elenbaas

Printed in the United States of America

First printing in 2014

To our sweet daughters, who have cheered us on through this process despite not knowing the full scope of this book. You are fiercely loved.

Contents

Why We Ever Thought This Might Be a Good Idea

This book is not a cure for your porn addiction or your spouse's. If we claimed to have all the answers within these pages, we'd be scamming you. What this book holds is our story. It's a story of hope. A story of grace. A story of a marriage restored. It's also a story of a lot of hard work, but it's effort well spent.

The more our society talks about the ugly secretiveness of pornography, the more we direct our attention to the battle that greatly needs our valiant efforts. Shying away from our own stories, no matter how much sin we must uncover to the world, only gives power to the one who seeks to destroy us. There is so much shame associated with porn addiction and so many of us, men and women, suffer in silence. We feel alone because very few are willing to stand up and say among people that we know that it is an issue in our homes. But you are not alone:

- In 2003, a Focus on the Family poll showed 47% percent of families said pornography is a problem in their home.[1]

- In 2004, 42% of surveyed adults indicated that their partner's use of pornography made them feel insecure, and 41% admitted that they felt less attractive due to their partner's pornography use.[2]

- In a 2008 study of college students aged 18–26, researchers found that 86% of young adult men reported having used pornography in the past year, with approximately one fifth reporting daily or every-other-day use and 48.4% reporting weekly pornography use.[3]

- In 1994, a survey showed 91% of men raised in Christian homes were exposed to pornography while growing up (compared to 98% of those not raised in a Christian home).[4]

- In August 2006, a survey reported 50% of all Christian men and 20% of all Christian women are addicted to pornography.[5]

It's easy to look on the outside of a family and think all is well. But there is a very real chance that the people inside are struggling with similar issues, just like you.

In this book, you will find our story. It is our prayer that you will read it with an open heart and a discerning spirit and that through our story, God will speak to you. We pray our story brings you hope, no matter how hopeless you may feel. We pray that all that is held in darkness will be brought to light. And we pray for you, no matter where you are in your journey, that you will hold fast to the hand of God, that your eyes will see as He sees, that your heart would be sheltered under the shadow of His wings.

A word about the structure of this book: There are many issues surrounding porn addiction and we have tried to address many of them here from both of our perspectives. As such, this book is informally divided into six parts, each one targeting a different issue related to porn addiction.

Each part has three chapters. The first chapter is told from Jen's perspective. Craig writes from his perspective in the second chapter. The third chapter is designed to help you as a couple work through whatever we have previously discussed. It is this third chapter where we primarily dig through Scripture and the available research and then ask you to converse with each other. It is our hope that the discussion questions in these chapters will provide an open space for you to share *your* perspective and heart with your partner.

We invite you both to read the whole book, not just the chapters you think would apply most to you. Part of the healing and recovery process of porn addiction is understanding where your spouse is coming from and how/why he/she got there in the first place. But don't assume your spouse feels just like Craig or Jen. Instead, use our stories as a point of departure to openly discuss yours.

PART 1

Discovering Darkness

CHAPTER 1

The Smoking Gun

For everything that is hidden will eventually be brought into the open, and every secret will be brought to light.

Mark 4:22

■ Her

"Do you ever look at porn?"

It was an impromptu question and the first time I ever asked my then boyfriend, Craig, about pornography. And to my casual question came a casual response: "Oh, I have in the past. Every guy does it."

I lumped his admission to previous porn use in with his ex-girlfriends—simple memories that could be stored in a mental shoebox on a closet shelf. I thought, with my twenty-year-old brain, that the past was the past and we were starting a brand-new, sparkling future. I used the fact that we were both sponsors of our church's youth group as insurance against pornography being any real threat. Surely any man who takes the time to invest in the spiritual lives of children would not be sucked into the under-world of pornography. And I rationalized that porn was some-thing that guys used because they didn't have a girl. Now, Craig had a girl—*me*—and I could fill any and all of those empty places in his heart. I would be able to meet his every need. There would be no room for anyone else, much less pictures and movies on the Internet. What could they give that I could not?

At some point early in our marriage, though, I began to suspect that the porn he had alluded to from his past was too big to fit in any shoebox. It wasn't something that had ever been shelved, and because of Craig's health scare that took place at the very start of our married life, it continued to provide a means of escape from the unknown realities of this world.

The night we arrived home from the second leg of our honeymoon, which consisted of traveling in two white Ford Econoline vans from Texas to New Mexico for the senior high school mission trip to the Navajo reservation, we received two letters from our life insurance company. A few weeks before we were married, we had both had physicals to qualify for life insurance. I opened my letter first and casually noted that I had been approved. Craig opened his letter next, revealing a very different outcome. He had been denied due to high protein levels in his urine. Immediately I thought my worst nightmare had come true—I would get married and then lose the man to whom I had given my heart. Frantically, I grabbed the phone book and called a local hospital. I talked to a nurse who graciously told me there was most likely no immediate emergency, but Craig should see a doctor soon. The next day, we began an adventure that would last the next five years. Urine collections, biopsy, and medications—oh my! Lest I leave you worried and wondering, Craig was finally diagnosed with glomerulonephritis and is now in total remission.

It became apparent early in those first few months of grappling with Craig's disease how differently he and I handled trials. My instinct was to try to take care of him—physically, emotionally, and mentally. I thought, as a new wife, my role was to be a supreme confidante, allowing him to vent and complain and strategize about tackling this unforeseen circumstance. I also thought I should take special care to keep his mind off this trouble, so I planned outings, parties, and romantic nights. While he seemed to enjoy the social activities, the romantic nights were another story. In bed, he often pushed me away, despite my persistent pursuits. When I asked him what was so wrong with me that he couldn't be with his new wife, he simply said that his medical issues weighed so heavily on his mind that he couldn't engage in that way with me. But at the same time he was rejecting my sexual advances in the bedroom, I also noticed an increase in the amount of time he was spending on the computer.

When I entered the room, often late at night when I realized he had left our bed, I saw how he switched the screen or closed a window on the computer. When I asked what he was doing, he would give me some mundane answer such as "just surfing the net." There were other curious clues that Craig's "surfing the net" was less than innocent. There was that stain on the cloth computer chair that wouldn't go away. Then there was the cable bill with a pay-per-view movie charge. Of course, since we had very little money, I called to see what the movie was, sure that there was some mistake and that we would be recouping the erroneous charge. Craig overheard me and before the agent could spit out the name of the porno movie, Craig told me it was some Samurai flick.

Craig had explanations for everything and they all sounded good enough. No wife wants to believe, based on circumstantial evidence, that her husband is obsessed by things that don't remotely resemble her. And no wife wants to know that despite all her efforts to please, she still plays second fiddle to some image that seems to get the job done.

But one day, all this circumstantial evidence became the smoking gun.

It took me two years to find it, but find it I did. I happened to look in the history on the computer, searching for something I needed for my teaching job, and all these URLs with explicit names appeared on the screen. I clicked on one and in my head thought, "I knew it!" But the validation of being right was quickly canceled out by the fact that I was right about something of which I wanted to be very, very wrong. I called Craig in immediately. "Is this the only site you've looked at?" He nodded his head "yes" but a click of another button revealed another story. I don't remember the number of websites or images I found that day, but I remember the feeling of my heart cracking open. I remember the shame on his face. I remember wondering if I could ever trust him again.

Somehow, we moved on from that night. I am sure that he told me he would never look at it again, that he didn't compare me with the intense images on the screen. I honestly believe that after seeing how much brokenness the pornography caused in our marriage that day, he didn't ever want to look at porn again. But as we discovered later, the porn had been such a way for him to escape the everyday pressures of life that he would not be able to stop on his own volition. The pornographic world was a world in which he was free from his stresses and responsibilities. It was a world in which he had no health problems, no pressure to perform, no possibilities of rejection. Pornography was his ticket to freedom. Or so he thought.

Just a few months after our first daughter was born, Craig hit rock bottom. He had gotten up with her in the morning, fed her, and put her back down for a nap. I woke up, found him in the study, and went ballistic. What few rules we had put in place since my first discovery (no doors closed, no minimizing windows when I walked in) had been broken. On top of that, I was nowhere near pre-baby body, so all those self-image and comparison issues came roaring back fiercely. There was no grace in my cutting words. I vented. I cursed at him. The questions came in a torrent:

"How could you do this to me?"

"Why can you not control yourself?"

"Don't you realize you have a daughter now?"

"How would you feel if that was her someday on that screen?"

"Am I just not good enough for you?"

That morning I could not contain the ugly black mess of my anger and insecurity. And my lack of grace and self-control covered his ugly black mess of addiction and disobedience to God. Suddenly, he was sinking in a dark sea of despair with no lifelines left. The next thing I knew, he threw on some old clothes and started walking out the door. I asked him what he was doing. He said that he was going to cut the grass so that I wouldn't have to worry about that for a while. Thoroughly confused, I asked him what he was talking about.

"You don't want me around anymore."

"You deserve better than this."

The conversation oscillated between him leaving our *family* so that he would no longer burden us with his problem and leaving this *world* so that he didn't burden himself with this problem. I felt the floor dropping out from underneath me. Simultaneously I was raging mad, insanely sad, and overwhelmed with fear. Functioning on little sleep due to our newborn child, I could not process all of this, much less make the situation any better. I am sure the only prayer I could formulate was something like, "Dear God, please help us." In actuality, most of the thoughts running around my brain centered on the fact that I might soon be a single mother.

While all this was happening, I forgot my mom was coming over to see the baby. At this point, I had gotten Craig back to the bedroom. He was lying on his side, weeping, and I was alternating between being stunned, praying for him, and keeping watch over our daughter. The doorbell rang and I ran to the door. I flung it open, burst into a new round of tears, handed my child to my mother, and blubbered out the words "Craig is addicted to porn. I caught him again this morning." I don't even remember her response because I headed back to the bedroom to call Craig's parents. As much as I didn't want them to know, I was out of gas and out of resources. Thankfully, his dad answered the phone and I filled him in about his suicidal son and briefed him about the events that led up to this crisis. Craig and his dad, an Episcopal priest, talked together for some time and by the end of the conversation, Craig seemed much more lucid and calm. One of the primary fruits from that conversation, aside from unconditional love from his parents, was that Craig should begin counseling.

Craig called the counselor his dad had recommended and we began anew in formulating rules and regulations that might serve to keep him accountable to his resolution of not engaging in porn. We flipped the desk in the study to the opposite wall so that the screen could be seen from the doorway. I checked his history daily (he was not supposed to delete anything) and bought him the *Every Man's Battle* book, complete with workbook. We started a couple's journal and studied some of the same passages of Scripture, reflecting on how God's Word was speaking to us. We discussed porn daily and I asked him over and over again if he was tempted that day and if so, what he did to overcome the temptation.

While things seemed to get better, there were still red flags. For example, when I would ask Craig about his once-a-week counseling sessions, he would often share with me how they got sidetracked on some sort of historical conversation that had no relevance to either him or the porn addiction. The counselor knew Craig's family well, which perhaps made it easy to fall into a more friendly relationship instead of a counselor-patient relationship. We didn't think about changing counselors because we couldn't afford to pay any more than we were paying and this man was giving us a huge discount. Even though it was clear to me that due to Craig's personable nature, the counselor easily fell prey to Craig's deflective strategies, we continued on with him because we didn't know what else to do.

I tried to tell Craig what was happening—to let him know that he wasn't fully engaging, but of course he knew this already. As much as I think he honestly wanted to get better, he wasn't able to let go of something that had been his security blanket for so long. He wasn't ready to trade the false world of pornography for a healthy relationship with his wife or with God.

At some point the counseling ended and we went on with our married life. I remained suspicious, no matter how much Craig tried to persuade me that he was okay. If he had the door closed to the study, I would try to open it quickly to catch him in the act. If I found the history cleared on a random day, I would ask him about it. But usually if he told me "it's good to empty the cache" I would accept his answer—at least to his face. The truth is, both of us were living in some form of denial, pretending real freedom had been found. I tried trusting him again when he said he was hardly ever tempted. I made myself believe that all my strategies had worked. I celebrated his freedom, claiming victory over pornography so it would be our new reality.

And then Mother's Day came.

Craig told me that I should splurge and go get a haircut. I drove to the salon, but it was closed because the shop owner was a new mother. Disappointed, I drove home, contemplating the next opportunity I might have to escape the house alone without my two little girls. When I walked in the door, my two-year-old was watching Elmo in the living room, unattended, the TV blaring. I could hear my six-month-old screaming from her crib. I figured my husband must be back there trying to get her down for a nap or changing her diaper, but when I walked in, there was no one in the room but her. I quickly picked her up and went to find my husband. Every hair stood up on the back of my neck. I was sick to my stomach because I knew what was happening behind the closed door to the office. You can guess what I found when I quickly opened the door. I'll spare you the details.

Rage doesn't quite adequately describe my feelings at the time. No longer was it just about him looking at naked girls and sex acts on the web, but now the addiction was overtaking his desire to be the loving, responsible father I knew he wanted to be. Pornography had ceased being just about marital infidelity. Its reach seemed ever increasing.

I felt powerless. I had tried everything I could think of to rid our lives of porn. I had bought him books. We arranged for counseling. I monitored his e-mail accounts, his web browser history, and his time on the computer. I drilled him, I questioned him, I cried out to him—*How could you do this to me?* Nothing had worked. And so, I went inside my bathroom closet, the farthest I could get from everyone, threw myself on the floor, and railed at God. I cursed at Him. I ranted.

"You picked him for me?"

"Why did you let me walk into this situation? Why didn't you protect me?"

"You know I have trust issues and he has failed me time and time again!"

"Can I trust him to be a father to two little girls?"

"Can I trust him to ever be a faithful husband?"

"Is anything I do or say going to work?"

Something broke in me after this tirade against God. I realized that Craig's captivity provided monstrous quantities of fuel that powered my desire to cure him, rehabilitate him, to help him become consumed with anything but porn. In that moment, I realized that we had both become enslaved. We were trapped by different chains, but they were chains nonetheless. They held us back from Jesus. They held us back from each other. They threatened to keep us seated in our own personal prisons forever.

As much as I prayed that God would heal him from his addiction, and as much as I knew that he could be set free, I simply had not let God handle this one on His own. In my mind, there were too many things at stake—my marriage, my husband's life, my children, my self-respect, his self-respect. Somehow, I had fooled myself into believing that becoming the porn police was going to ensure successful recovery. Somehow, I had fallen into the trap of believing that if I said and did the right things, healing would take place. I couldn't help but try to orchestrate the whole process, because I felt if I didn't get control over this situation, everything as I knew it would fall apart. Crumble. Cease to exist.

I focused all my energy on what he was doing and why he was doing it. In the process, I simply forgot to do two very important things:

Trust God.

Respect my husband.

In my attempt to control, I forgot to surrender. I forgot to let God work. I forgot to let God heal. I forgot that Craig belonged to Him and not just to me. In the end, I became blinded by the enormity of the problem instead of boasting of the immensity of God's power. Chains have a way of making you forget the power of the One you serve.

In the darkness of that moment, God brought light, showing me that I had I lost sight of my husband. I began to define him by what he was doing instead of who God created him to be. Perhaps even more revealing was the notion that I had lost sight of God's power and His place in our lives. I had strapped on the burden of "healer" when I should have been showing humility, bowing low to the One who can do all things.

On the floor of the bathroom closet was the turning point— both in my relationship with my husband and my relationship with God.

CHAPTER 2

Back to the Beginning

"For my people have done two evil things: They have abandoned me—the fountain of living water. And they have dug for themselves cracked cisterns that can hold no water at all!"[1]

Jeremiah 2:13

■ Him

When I started writing this chapter I immediately wanted to describe my first experiences with pornography. But it just didn't seem *right* to start there. I thought about it, struggled with it, and finally prayed about it. The problem was that I was starting in the middle of the story. There is much more to me than just porn addiction. You need the backstory. You need context. So . . . I'll start at the beginning.

I was born and raised in the great state of Louisiana. For the first sixteen years of my life, every house I lived in was within a geographical circle of five miles. My family and I lived "out in the parish" as they say, meaning beyond the city limits. But it was really just the suburbs where the neighborhoods are similar—the same three-bedroom, two-bath houses, the same white, middle class, nuclear families. Woods and bayous surrounded the neighborhoods, so happily for me it was a suburb with a rural vibe.

I am a child of the '80s, raised on pop culture. Playtime was Transformers, GI Joes, and BB guns. (No, I never shot my eye out. Well, there was my best friend's knee, but that's another story.) Countless bayou critters fell prey to my ninja-like stealth and firearm prowess.

My childhood was lived mostly outdoors. Mom and Dad didn't tolerate a lot of TV time. That was reserved for after dinner. I'm sure many of you have heard the familiar phrase, "It's such a beautiful day! Why don't you go outside and play?" That was parent-speak for "You're driving me crazy! Please go away!" But that was just fine with me. I enjoyed being outside with my friends. I loved the sense of freedom and independence.

As long as I can remember I've had an active imagination. This is important because it plays into my addiction. But during early childhood, I used my imagination to make the games my friends and I played a lot more fun. This was the time of *Rambo* and *Missing in Action*. The woods of the bayou suddenly became the jungles of Vietnam. My friends and I were Army Rangers on a mission to rescue prisoners of war. Our BB guns became our trusted M-16s and the birds, snakes, squirrels, or whatever animal we could find were the dreaded Viet Cong. To outsiders, it may have resembled *Lord of Flies*, but to us it was awesome!

Both of my parents worked away from the home. My dad was a traveling salesman and my mom was an administrative assistant (back then she was called a secretary). Dad traveled often on business. When he was in town, he worked the typical 8 a.m. to 5 p.m. workday, as did Mom. This meant that after school from 3 p.m. to 5:30 or so, my siblings and I were on our own.

Let me give you a snapshot of my family dynamics. I have an older brother and a younger sister. Both of my siblings have outgoing personalities, much like my father. I on the other hand am much more reserved, like my mother. My dad and siblings would drive the conversations while my mom and I listened and responded when we felt like it.

Our school-year routine was to come home and do our homework, and then my sister and I would start making dinner. We usually ate together as a family. This is something that Jen and I have carried on in our family, and I think it is one of the most important activities we as parents can do with our kids. Nothing bonds a family quite like a shared meal.

Because I often felt overshadowed in the daily conversations that took place during my childhood around the dinner table and beyond, I began to keep the hard questions and true struggles to myself.

In addition to traveling for work, Dad was also a member of the Army Reserves. That meant he was gone one weekend a month and two weeks in the summer. Now that I'm a husband and father, I know that must have been hard on him. As I look back now through my husband/father lens, I see where he did his best to make up for lost time. He showed up to football games, art shows, and dance recitals. He planned and participated in family activities. I know he tried hard, but I still remember wanting more time with him. I think every kid wants that.

It wasn't until later that I began to develop a strong relationship with my dad. While I was in high school, we moved to Texas so that Dad could attend seminary. My whole life had been Monroe, Louisiana. Now we were moving to Austin. As it turned out, the move was a great opportunity and an adventure. I have made lifelong friends here and met my wife, Jennifer. Not too bad for a redneck boy from the bayou.

After the move, my dad would often drop me off at school or work. During those car rides I had him all to myself. I still remember those conversations. I hadn't realized up to that point *how much* I wanted that time with him. I began to see my dad in a completely different light. It occurred to me that I craved this relationship with my daddy.

One morning, I began to open up to him about the culture shock I had experienced in the move. No longer was it the status quo to be a Christian and go to church. Instead, I met people who wanted to explore anything *but* Christianity. My dad observed, "You'll find people often search for a religion that fits their preferred lifestyle, instead of transforming their lifestyle to fit their religion." I had always thought of my dad as smart, but I hadn't grasped the extent of his wisdom.

My relationship with my dad has continued to evolve. He's been there to provide words of encouragement and advice as I've navigated through marriage and fatherhood. I'm extremely thankful that God has helped this relationship grow.

Despite the great improvement in my relationship with my father, one thing lacked. We didn't talk about sex, masturbation, or pornography. In fact, no adult gave me advice about this. Once these things entered my life, I had no one to show me boundaries or the way to go.

My earliest recollection of porn was in sixth grade. A friend's father had a subscription to *Playboy*. My friend routinely sneaked the magazines out of his house and we would take them out into the woods. I never brought them home and we only looked at them when we were in our fort in the woods. I remember being excited by the images of these women. It started as simple curiosity, but I knew it was wrong and I wanted to keep it secret. At the time, I had no idea that this secret would foster a stronger desire to seek out more images and that they would continue to prey on my young adult male curiosity.

When I was in junior high, a friend's older brother was in high school and, unbeknown to him, we gained access to his porn video library. When he was not at home we would sneak into his room to watch them on his TV or covertly take them out only to return them before he would realize that they were missing.

During this time I found my grandfather's stash of pornography hidden in one of his filing cabinets. Many late nights I would sneak into his office to pilfer a videotape and watch it on his VCR or "borrow" a magazine to take home only to never to return it.

In a study conducted by Ohio State University, researchers found that on average men think or fantasize about sex nineteen times a day versus the ten times a day for women.[2] I may have been an overachiever. Even though I had access to pornography, it didn't have to be a porn magazine or movie. I didn't have to have porn material in order to masturbate. It could be a catalog, advertisement, anything that showed a scantily clad female. Even if I didn't readily have access to something visual, I could make it up.

This is where my imagination was not my friend. I would fantasize about girls from school, church, wherever. Often the ages of the girls were my age but sometimes they were older. I also fantasized about a couple of teachers as well.

In an especially bad development, I became sexually active at an early age. I lost my virginity in the seventh grade. It was a horrible experience. At the time, I had a very nice and attractive girlfriend. Yet I had sex with a *different* girl—one with a bad reputation around school. She bragged about drinking and having sex on a regular basis.

It happened during a campout at a friend's house. The girl had come over with a few of her friends who had been drinking that day. She was obviously drunk and very "handsy" with me. I had never had a drink in my life and had no intentions prior to that time to do anything with her. She, however, had it in mind to have sex with me. She pulled me into a room and started kissing me and things progressed from there. I could have stopped but for some reason I didn't.

This mistake would haunt me for years. I tried to minimize what had happened, but the truth is that sex between two people in such circumstances is always traumatic, regardless of the denial we may tenaciously cling to.

In fact, the entire incident may well have worsened my problem with porn and masturbation. I felt tremendous shame, and I needed a place to retreat and find comfort. My independent spirit drove me to porn.

After masturbating, I would feel embarrassed or ashamed by what I was doing, especially as I got older. By now I was a leader in the church and felt that it was wrong to fantasize about having sex with women who were not my wife, but I could never seem to stop.

When I first starting working, I occasionally visited a porn video outlet to buy videos and magazines. These visits were infrequent and almost always on impulse. But when I gained access to a computer and the Internet, my porn viewing reached a whole new level.

Once I had access to the Internet, I could view pictures or videos in the comfort of my own home and with complete anonymity. I didn't have to worry about someone seeing my car parked in front of a store. I could look at it anytime I wanted. The source material was endless, as was my hunger for it.

This went on even after Jen and I got married. I struggled to keep it hidden, but you can only keep a secret like that for so long, especially from your wife.

Through several cycles of failure and recovery, I've come to realize that I have a problem. It's an addiction to pornography. It's been my problem for a long time, and now I've made it my family's problem. I've used pornography as a means to cope with the pain and stress of life. The feelings that I'm referring to are the same ones that all of us feel in this broken world. Have you ever felt like you weren't measuring up? Have you ever felt the sting of jealousy that someone else was smarter, faster, more attractive? Sure! We all have.

As a child I learned that when I felt that way, I could make myself feel good whenever I wanted. I didn't have to rely on anyone else. Pornography became a means of escape. In the fantasy, I could be anyone, have anyone, and do anything. It didn't matter what was going on in my "real" life. I could always retreat there and find comfort. However, I came to realize that it's all a lie.

Perhaps you have a similar story. Was your wife cleaning and accidently found the hidden "stash"? Did your girlfriend see your computer and find something after you forgot to wipe the browsing history? Or maybe she noticed that you *had* erased the history, and now she wonders why. Maybe you forgot to take the DVD out of the player. Or maybe you haven't been caught yet, but the guilt is eating you alive.

The Bible has a parallel story. It's seen in the ancient Israelites, who bear a remarkable resemblance to me.

Most of us know the stories. Time and again, God promised to care for His people. And He always came through, caring for them in miraculous ways.

He did it with the series of plagues against Egypt, whose leader, Pharaoh, was enslaving the Israelites. He did it when the entire nation was trapped at the shores of the Red Sea with Pharaoh's army closing in. He gave them water from the desert rock and manna from heaven every day. He conquered their enemies for them. But God's people didn't trust Him. They complained. They whined. They murmured. And they looked for comfort and relief apart from God. They rejected Him.

This pattern with Israel continued for centuries. Eventually, God gave Jeremiah the prophet this heart-breaking message: "My people have done two evil things: They have abandoned me—the fountain of living water. And they have dug for themselves cracked cisterns that can hold no water at all!" (Jeremiah 2:13).

Just like the ancient Israelites, I rejected God and His love. I tried to do things my own way. I desired acceptance, but I pretended not to care how others felt about me. I needed love, but I chose to chase after a false sense of self-reliance. Throughout my life, God has always been beside me, seeking me out, calling after me. But instead of reaching out to the source of eternal living water, I too dug dry cisterns with my bare hands that could not hold water.

If I am going to lead my wife and kids, I must first allow myself to be led by God. It's not that I'm going to be sinless or never make a mistake. But I want to cultivate the desire to be pure and to live according to God's will, not my own cravings.

I cannot do this on my own. I cannot hide in my house, locked in a room away from everything in the world. When Jesus prayed to His heavenly Father the night before He was crucified, he said, "The world hates them [his followers] because they do not belong to the world, just as I do not belong to the world. I'm not asking you to take them out of the world, but to keep them safe from the evil one" (John 17:14–15).

Porn is in the world, and it has become mainstream. What used to be kept in seedy theaters on the wrong side of town is now center stage and prime time. Not only are we exposed to it constantly, so are our children.

But it doesn't have to defeat us! Jesus also said, "Take heart, because I have overcome the world" (John 16:33). His friend and disciple John later assured us, "Every child of God defeats this evil world, and we achieve this victory through our faith. And who can win this battle against the world? Only those who believe that Jesus is the Son of God" (1 John 5:4–5).

God shows us a better way to live. A way of purity. A way of holiness. A way of truth.

But to live this way requires Jesus. And it doesn't hurt to share the journey with a wife who loves Jesus, too.

CHAPTER 3

Is Pornography Really Dangerous?

These desires give birth to sinful actions. And when sin is allowed to grow, it gives birth to death.

James 1:15

How often have you engaged in behavior you knew to be wrong, but when asked why you did it, your first reaction was to justify your actions? We all do it. We all desire to do what we want and we want it to be right. We try to rationalize our behavior so we don't feel bad about it.

Craig looked for a way to frame things so he could still engage with pornography and not feel *as* guilty (because it's very hard for him to deny the conviction of the Holy Spirit *entirely*). What are you saying to yourself and to your spouse? If you are the one struggling with using porn, perhaps you can relate to some of the lies Craig bought into, such as:

- "God does not specifically mention pornography in the Bible, so how can it be that dangerous?"

- "I'm not really betraying my spouse—that involves actual sex with another person."

- "I can sin now and ask forgiveness later."

- "If it were so bad, there wouldn't be so many people putting this stuff out there and so many people using it."

- "I know other Christians who use it."

Jen also had a way of using her own excuses to continue denying the destructive power of porn in her marriage. If you are in a similar situation, perhaps you've said something like this:

- "At least he is not actually touching another woman."

- "I'm sure lots of husbands are doing the very same thing."

- "If I can just lose twenty pounds, he'll find me as attractive as they are. Then, he'll stop."

- "If I say anything else about it, he'll just tell me I'm nagging him and it will make him want to do it more often."

Do any of these excuses or rationalizations sound familiar?

Essentially, to rationalize is to suppress the truth or keep it hidden in places where we can pretend not to see it. Imagine yourself in a car, driving down the road. Ahead, you see a detour in your lane. There is a barricade with a warning sign, but you could easily veer your car around it without going into oncoming traffic. For a moment, you consider: *Is it safe to continue driving down this road like I had planned?* Then, the rationales come:

- Wouldn't they have put more barricades up if it were *really* unsafe?

- Those construction people—they always make a big deal out of the smallest things. I'm sure I'll be just fine.

The truth is, you want to get where you are going and you don't want to be denied getting there on time or as fast as you can. So you take a risk to fulfill those desires. But what happens when you find out that your rationale for avoiding the blockades and the warnings don't hold up?

You fall in a sinkhole. You wreck your car and your body. You might even end up hurting someone else.

Pornography rationalizations are the same way—they don't hold up against God's truth and His ways. If you choose to believe the rationalizations, even for a moment, it's like driving your car around the barricades, ignoring the warning signs, and falling into a pit.

How can pornography equate to a big, black hole in the road? How can it really be as dangerous as driving a car past barricades? True, the Bible does not specifically address pornography as we know it today (viewing pictures of naked women, or sex on the television, computer, or in magazines, among other things), but if we get to the heart of what pornography is about, we find something that is mentioned over and over again—lust. We all have an understanding of how the world defines lust, but what does God say about lusting?

"But I say to you that everyone who looks at a woman with lustful intent has already committed adultery with her in his heart." (Matthew 5:28 ESV)

Ouch. These words from Jesus cut straight to the heart of the matter. If you look at adultery purely from a secular definition, it involves sexual intercourse between a married person and someone other than his/her spouse. But Jesus looks beyond the physical act of betrayal. He accounts for the state of the heart.

When we look at pornography, we make a conscious decision to go outside the marriage for sexual fulfillment and release, even if they are simply images on a screen. These images (whether still photographs or actual video of sex acts) may seem harmless because there is no emotional attachment between the engager and the seducers. However, the pornography user forms an attachment to the *use* of pornography, which is the act of lusting.

Like addictive drugs, pornography offers a high and keeps the user coming back for more. Sexual release activates hormones such as endorphins and epinephrine. When these flood the body due to porn use, a physiological correlation between watching porn and feeling good is established, leading porn users to want to engage more often. Drug addicts often have to take more drugs to achieve the same high. Porn addicts are the same way. Their "more" may come in the form of increased viewing, seeking out more extreme levels of pornography ("hard core" versus "soft core"), or even seeking to act out these fantasy engagements in the flesh. Mary Anne Layden, PhD, a psychotherapist and Director of Education at the Center for Cognitive Therapy at the University of Pennsylvania, writes about porn:

> The Internet is a perfect drug delivery system because you are anonymous, aroused and have role models for these behaviors. To have [the] drug pumped into your house 24/7, free, and children know how to use it better than grown-ups know how to use it—it's a perfect delivery system if we want to have a whole generation of young addicts who will never have the drug out of their mind.[1]

How does what we do with our bodies affect our emotions and our hearts? Consider these scientifically researched conclusions:

- *There is a correlation between the amount of porn one views and the measure of satisfaction real sex brings.* One online survey showed that the more porn a man engaged with, the less fulfillment his real sex life brought him and the less he initiated sex with his partner.[2]

- *Viewing pornography hinders relationship-building skills.*[3] Real relationships have problems, conflicts, and issues. If we are used to living in a fantasy world where these types of things do not occur, it skews our perspective about what relationships entail and gives us unrealistic expectations of other people.

- *People who have cheated on their spouse were three times more likely to have engaged with Internet pornography.*[4] Pornography can lead to the physical act of adultery. Major red flag.

Jesus' words in the book of Matthew may seem extreme in our society, but the research shows that permitting lust in our thoughts can lead to behaviors that destroy our relationships. If we return to our "hole in the road" analogy, we know there are barriers to keep us from the danger ahead. What we don't know is the size of the danger. It's the same with pornography and lust. We don't know how far we will fall if we ignore the blockades. Better to heed the warning, change our course, and avoid the pit altogether. The payoff is never worth the danger.

Temptation comes from our own desires, which entice us and drag us away. These desires give birth to sinful actions. And when sin is allowed to grow, it gives birth to death. So don't be misled, my dear brothers and sisters. (James 1:14–16)

You may dabble in porn occasionally and not think any of the scientifically researched conclusions apply to you. Perhaps this makes your pit look shallow, even inconsequential. But being in any pit, giving in to any lust, carries us away from fellowship with God. This separation from God is exactly the reason that Satan attempts to lead us astray at every turn in our lives, wooing us closer and closer to things that God has told us are not for us.

We see this from the very beginning of time, played out in the garden of Eden. The same words Satan whispers in your heart are born of the same fruit as the words he told Eve. "'You won't die!' the serpent replied to the woman. 'God knows that your eyes will be opened as soon as you eat it, and you will be like God, knowing both good and evil'" (Genesis 3:4–5). And in a sense, Satan was right—Adam and Eve did not physically die (at least not immediately), but part of their relationship with God did. Satan is also right when he tells us that if we experience pornography, our eyes will be open to new things and new ideas. What he doesn't tell us is that the sin of engaging with these new things will bring about separation from God. The truth is stark—God has equated lust with sin, and sin with death.

In his first letter to the Corinthians, Paul dealt with sexual immorality and the threat it posed to the church. After listing all kinds of sexual sins (1 Corinthians 6:9), he wrote, "Some of you were once like that. But you were cleansed; you were made holy; you were made right with God by calling on the name of the Lord Jesus Christ and by the Spirit of our God" (v. 11). But Paul still worried about the behavior of the Christians in Corinth. And so he added, "You can't say that our bodies were made for sexual immorality. They were made for the Lord, and the Lord cares about our bodies" (v. 13).

When we participate in immoral behavior, Paul said it is like taking our bodies and joining them with a prostitute. He writes, "Don't you realize that if a man joins himself to a prostitute, he becomes one body with her? For the Scriptures say, *'The two are united into one'*" (v. 16, emphasis mine). Jesus said that God designed marriage to be a unification of two bodies into one. Quoting the Old Testament, He told the Pharisees, "'God made them male and female' from the beginning of creation. 'This explains why a man leaves his father and mother and is joined to his wife, and the two are united into one'" (Mark 10:6–8).[5] Throughout Scripture, the institution of marriage repeatedly shows up as an analogy for our relationship with Christ. It makes sense, then, to conclude that what negatively affects our marital unions also affects our spiritual union with Christ.

God knows our weakness and the power of evil. He knows Satan desires to deceive us and lead us astray. And so He not only lovingly gives us His Word with its cautions, but He also equips us with other tools, enabling us to fight back against these rationalizations for porn use.

How do we know even know He desires to protect us from the lies of Satan? Second Thessalonians 3:3 says, "But the Lord is faithful; he will strengthen you and guard you from the evil one." In the Psalms, we find countless pleas on behalf of various psalmists for God to be their protector. "Sustain me, and I will be rescued; then I will meditate continually on your decrees," wrote David (119:117). Throughout the Old Testament, we find stories of how God led His people out of slavery into a land of promise: "The LORD went ahead of them. He guided them during the day with a pillar of cloud, and he provided light at night with a pillar of fire" (Exodus 13:21).

Just as we need a highway authority to show us when our paths contain dangers ahead, we need God's Word to show us those potential pitfalls on our spiritual journeys as well. When God tells us to stay away from something, we must trust that He is acting in our best interest. He is not denying us the things we want, but rather saving us from bondage that ravages our souls, our relationship with God, and our marriages.

If God's Word is the barricade that warns us that destruction lies ahead, the Holy Spirit is our guide, leading us to paths that bring real fulfillment. The Holy Spirit is an active and alive presence in our lives who nudges us when we are heading the wrong direction and helps us choose wisely. He desires for us to use our bodies to honor God and to keep union with Him. Jesus says: "When the Spirit of truth comes, he will guide you into all truth. He will not speak on his own but will tell you what he has heard. He will tell you about the future" (John 16:13).

Here is good news: If you are the one engaging with pornography and you feel the war within your soul, you are sensing the Holy Spirit! Recognizing that pornography is not a useful tool to bring fulfillment to your life is the very work of the Holy Spirit in you. This is hope! This is something to celebrate. Don't simply focus on the daily struggle with porn. There is a beginning to every process and you may well be at the beginning of yours.

Beware that Satan's voice starts interjecting at this crossroads as well—the place where you acknowledge the wrongdoing and decide to move toward purity. While the Holy Spirit convicts us, Satan tries to condemn us, sending us down a different pit, one of of darkness and despair.

Take this to your heart: "So now there is no condemnation for those who belong to Christ Jesus" (Romans 8:1). Write it on your mirror. Highlight it in your Bible. Memorize it with your spouse. God's Word protects you from Satan's pits.

What is the difference between convicting and condemning words?

Conviction sounds like . . .	Condemnation sounds like . . .
"You sinned out of your weakness when you looked at porn. But My power works best in weakness."[6]	"You looked at porn again. Told you that you can't get better. God will never be able to use you."
"You are weak when you don't trust in Me. I can and will supply all your needs."[7]	"You are really weak. You won't be able to resist it next time either."
"Let no one split apart what God has joined together.[8] Pornography comes in between you and your wife, but there is freedom from this bondage in Me."	"You should probably just get a divorce or move out. Your wife deserves so much better than you."

"The Holy Spirit comes to wake us up," Bishop Andy Doyle said one morning in church. It was Pentecost Sunday at our church, the yearly celebration of the arrival of the Holy Spirit, our Advocate.

Bishop Doyle said this after discussing the futuristic movie, *The Matrix*. Neo, the protagonist, when given a choice between two colored pills with different effects, chooses to take the red pill, committing himself to experience life for what it truly entails and forsaking the ignorant bliss of his current worldview. Just as the red pill opened his senses to a new reality, so can the Holy Spirit do this for us, Doyle explains. The Holy Spirit wakes us up to the fallacies of our rationalizations and shows us a different way. Satan tries to deceive us, luring us down roads paved with destruction, all the while convincing us that there really is no better way to meet our needs. Satan makes the way look smooth and easy, disguising the pitfalls and illuminating only the pleasurable things along the journey.

The Holy Spirit plays no tricks. It can be a hard road back to Christ. The very act of breaking out of chains is painful, but the Holy Spirit also reminds us that we do not go at it alone. We have a guide, a counselor, always at our side so that when we grow weary, we have strength. When we fall in despair, we have hope. When we feel lost, we have light. The Holy Spirit gently nudges us back from death to life, a process made possible by Jesus.

For you to discuss together:

1. What do you think about the statistics mentioned throughout chapter 3? Do they apply to you? If so, how? Do you and your spouse notice any correlation between the stats and your relationship?

2. Before you read this chapter, did you equate porn use with adultery? Why or why not? Has your view changed after reading the Scripture? How so?

3. What do you think about the role of the Holy Spirit in your life? How do you see the Holy Spirit moving in your life?

4. What are your views about pornography now that you have read the first three chapters? How have they changed? What is still the same?

PART 2

Encountering Light

CHAPTER 4

Illusions and Light

Let them praise the LORD for his great love
and for the wonderful things he has done for them.
For he satisfies the thirsty
and fills the hungry with good things.

Psalm 107:8–9

■ Her

If your husband is looking at pornography and you think, *If I could just look like that woman, he would only have eyes for me,* I'd like you to reconsider what your goals really are.

It's fantastic that you want to look good for your husband and be pleasing to him, but the image you are seeing on the computer or in the magazines has been perfectly molded to fit what the editors think will be the most eye-catching to any guy. If you are chasing a perfect body, you will be running for a long time. Long as in *eternity*, friend.

When Craig and I met, I was nineteen and had far from the perfect body. The Freshman Fifteen soon turned into the Sophomore Twenty. And yet, he was still attracted to me. He even wanted to marry me! Just a little tidbit about us: we got engaged eleven days after our first date, so he wasn't waiting to see if I would improve with age. And the truth is I didn't. At least not at first.

The first year we were married, I commuted forty-five miles one way to San Antonio, Monday through Friday, to finish my master's degree. He commuted about thirty miles every day in Austin traffic to work at his job. We had very little money, so a special date night consisted of eating at Whataburger. Needless to say, we didn't eat well and we didn't make much time for exercise.

Fast forward a few years. By now we had bought a house and were both working jobs considerably closer to our home. We had the time and money to begin focusing on our health. Okay, so health was secondary—I just wanted to be able to fit into cute maternity clothes since we had started talking about having a baby. And so I started exercising and eating Lean Cuisine to teach myself portion control. I began praying about my previous eating habits and wondering why I had allowed myself to become unhealthily overweight in the first place. Just before I started this journey of weight-loss, I went on a walk specifically to talk to God about my insatiable need for food.

Through prayer and introspection, God revealed to me that I was using food to fill a void in my life. I craved the feeling of fullness, and when I feared that there would not be enough to satisfy me I would break out in needless anxiety. Food has always been plentiful for me. I have never spent a day of my life destitute, without the means to purchase food to nourish my body. So even though I had no practical reason to fear that I would be without, my psychological need for food sent me messages that told me otherwise. I used food throughout my entire life to help me feel physically full when all I really wanted was to feel emotionally and spiritually full. Until I let God into those parts of my life, I would continue to fill my emptiness with tangible things that would not sustain me for the long haul.

Why all of a sudden have I started talking about food when you thought this book was going to be all about porn addiction? Two reasons:

1. Shrinking Jen ≠ Shrinking Porn Use

When Craig used porn, I believed that he thought those women on the screen were clearly more beautiful, more attractive, and sexier than I was. I thought they captured what he really wanted: perfect hair, perfect skin, perfectly big breasts. And always the sultry, pouty looks. I could never master that skill. How do I know? I've practiced. I always look weird.

I spent unfathomable amounts of brain space comparing myself to the images on the screen. In that competition, I always came up short. You see, my hair is curly underneath, wavy in the middle, and pretty much straight on top. My skin is prone to pimples, and big breasts were just never in the genetic cards for me. Adding to the breast "problem," I took up running to help me lose weight. If you are a woman, you know that the first place you don't want to lose weight is where you probably will.

I've run three marathons, as well as a good number of half-marathons, and lots of small races. I run three times a week and try to sneak in yoga when I can. I've managed my eating habits relatively well, and I am in a normal, healthy weight range. I've discovered the flat iron for my hair and switched my facial products. In short, I think I look much better after having two children than I ever did in the early years of our marriage.

However, despite all of these outward improvements, Craig still used porn. My hypothesis that my shrinking weight would equal shrinking porn use went out the window. Instead of realizing that his porn addiction was not about how *I* looked, I simply resigned myself to thinking that I was a failure. I would never be good enough so his eyes didn't wander. I wouldn't be the sole source of his satisfaction. I wouldn't be more desirable than the girl on the screen. Despite my best efforts, I could not rid myself of cellulite, wrinkles, and bad hair days. I would never look like an airbrushed beauty, and I couldn't afford the surgery that I thought it would take to make me into one.

It was a crushing blow to me to spend so much time and energy trying to fix both myself and Craig's porn problem and not get results. I spent my life learning that if you tried hard enough, you could get some sort of attention and acclaim. Even though I was never in the talented and gifted program, I tried hard in school and I got good grades. Even though I never won any races, I tried hard in running and I got faster. Even though I was never in the coolest, most popular crowd, I tried hard to be a good friend and I had a great social life.

There was always this nagging desire, though, to be *the best* in something, or if not the best, at least one of the front-runners. Yet I never felt like I arrived at this destination in anything that I tried, no matter how much effort I put into it. And now, in my marriage, I couldn't even be *the one* my husband desired, no matter if I lost weight, improved my hair, or mastered some pouty look. There was always someone who could look and act better.

I was so consumed at this point by how I didn't measure up that I didn't realize the people with whom I was competing had an incredibly unfair advantage. They got to hide all their less than desirable parts. Not with clothes, mind you, but with computer tools. The invention of Photoshop has completely altered what we as a society think is attractive, healthy, and appealing.

When digital retouching became the norm in the late 90s/early 2000s, our bodily ideal for women began to change, too. A lot of the things that got Photoshopped out of these Victoria's Secret images—folds of skin . . . , expression lines, traces of body hair, the texture of her skin—were visible in ad campaigns for global brands and on fashion magazine covers even as recently as the 1990s. We did not always think of the place where the pectoral muscle meets the armpit as something "ugly" in need of "fixing." We did not always think that it looked "bad" for a woman to squint slightly in the sun.[1]

Realizing the playing field wasn't level was helpful for several reasons. One, it helped me to understand that competing with people who appeared on a computer screen was dumb. In that world, they had magic wands. In my world, I didn't. Plus, I had two kids, a house, a husband, and part-time jobs. Trust me, if I could have wielded a magic wand, I would have.

Second, I came to the realization that even without computer editing, many of these women are physically beautiful. But so what? Do I really want to spend all my time trying to measure up to the ever-changing standards of this world? Is my external beauty my defining characteristic? Is physical beauty really the lynchpin that holds a marriage together? I think you and I both know this is not true.

Third, I wondered if any of these models and porn actors would choose to not have their good looks. I wondered if any of them would want to be anywhere but where they were when they were creating porn movies. I wondered if these beautiful women knew they were broken. After doing some research, I wept. Not for me anymore, but for them.

It's easy to be jealous. It's easy to think, "What if I had what they have?" It's harder, especially when you feel they have wronged you in some way (i.e., tantalizing your spouse), to be compassionate. I give you this next set of information not to devalue your anger, but to help you put your anger in its rightful place. As Paul writes in Ephesians, "For we are not fighting against flesh-and-blood enemies, but against evil rulers and authorities of the unseen world, against mighty powers in this dark world, and against evil spirits in the heavenly places" (6:12).

Your war is not against your body. It is not against porn stars. It is not against your husband. *It is against the powers of this dark world.*

Shelley Lubben is a former porn actress and founder of The Pink Cross Foundation, which helps women escape the porn industry. On her website she lists some shocking facts about people trapped in this exploitative business:

- Out of 1,500 performers working in California, 41 people *that she knows of* have died from AIDS, suicide, homicide, or drug-related deaths between 2007 and 2011.

- The average life expectancy of a porn performer is only 37.43 years. The average American lives to be 78.1 years old.

- The US adult film industry earns $9–$13 billion annually. Performers make $400–$1,000 per shoot and are not compensated based on distribution or sales.

- Porn stars are ten times more likely to have STDs. There are no laws in the porn industry that require performers to be tested for STDs.[2]

If the statistics are just numbers to you, let's bring in some words from the mouths of porn stars. Richard Pacecho, a retired porn star, said, "I think I had to become a sex star just to come back to normal because I had been so humiliated by being the fat kid. I had the largest breasts in the seventh grade . . . Do you know how deep those scars go?"[3] And Crissy Moran said, "I can't do anything else. This is what I'm good at."[4]

Seeing behind the veil of the pornography industry broke my heart. So often the people who get into this industry do so because they are desperate for attention, money, or self-worth. In the gentlest of voices, I ask you, sweet reader, if you've ever been desperate and made a decision that you might go back and change? Maybe the porn star on the screen and the two of us sitting here right now aren't so different? Sure, we've made different choices, but there have been lots of times when we didn't choose Jesus to satisfy our desires. Which leads me to why I had started talking about my food addiction in the first place . . .

2. Common Denominators

Craig and I are very different in myriad ways, but both of us are prone to addictive behaviors. Mine centered on food, and as you'll learn about later, control. His revolved around porn.

God is so faithful not to waste one bit of our experiences. Nearly everything that God revealed to me about my own food addiction, He used to help me understand Craig's porn addiction. Through my addiction, God showed me:

- *My addiction started because I had unmet needs.* I have vivid memories as a kid of sitting in the kitchen, my chair pulled up to the little television, and my hands continually diving into the cookie jar while I mindlessly watched TV. Food became a way to soothe my boredom and comfort me in distress. The times I most often turned to food were when I felt friendless, insecure, and without ability to control the situations around me. I desired something that would always be there and have an instantaneous effect. Food met both of these requirements. It was always in my house and enabled me to reach a point in which I felt a physical sense of satisfaction.

- *If I gave God my addiction, He would meet my needs.* Here is where addiction gets tricky. After I released my emotional attachment to food in order to lose weight, I could have easily found something else to fill the void that food used to fill. I could have become a neurotic exerciser or taken to skinny margaritas. It took intentional communion with God to help me avoid falling into another form of addiction. The process of examining why I ate and what compelled me to eat brought me to the underlying realization that nothing other than my relationship with God could bring me long-lasting security. Everything in this world had the potential to fail me. He never would. And here's the thing: I had to learn that life was not always going to be comfortable and it wasn't necessary for me to have to live in a state where I could manage everything. The trials we endure on this earth are here because they are simply what drive us closer to God. I have a yoga DVD made by Jillian Michaels where she says, "You have to get comfortable with being uncomfortable." It can be absolutely unnerving sitting there feeling out of control and not automatically running toward something of this world that will soothe your hurt soul. But when we make the space to wait and invite God in, real changes can happen within us and within the relationships around us. We have to push through the discomfort in order to be secure in the fact that God will catch us when we start to fall.

- *Bringing things to the light instead of hiding them in the dark is worth the risk.* The more I was honest with people about the whole process of my weight loss, the more I was able to keep front and center the heart of the issue—that I desperately needed God in order to be successful. I could have told people I was just dieting and exercising to lose weight. But it wasn't just that. I was now allowing God to show me my unhealthiness and teach me how to walk through life with His constant presence. I needed God to teach me how and why He is trustworthy. I had to learn that I am beautiful because He created me, not because of a number on the scale. I had to cultivate a habit of daily prayer so that I would remember that He is God, and He is in control of all things so I don't have to be. Bringing issues that had been following me since childhood into the light enabled me to be free of so many more issues than just being overweight.

Through some of the hardest days, nights, weeks, months, and years that we struggled with Craig's porn addiction, God kept bringing to mind that we are all guilty at some point of turning to something other than Him to fill the holes created by our imperfect world. This is the definition of sin.

Pornography is a hole-filler. If I can look at Craig and see that his addiction started just like mine—with unmet needs—I am able to have much more compassion, empathy, and grace. Bringing my own issues to the light brought freedom and hope and enabled me to move past the shame of pornography to talk about it openly with him and others.

CHAPTER 5

Delusions and Hope

Humble yourselves before God. Resist the devil,
and he will flee from you.

James 4:7

■ Him

I had been caught again, even though I had been careful. *Really* careful. At least, I thought I had been. But despite my best covert measures, Jen had caught me engaging with pornography. She was supposed to be gone to a hair appointment. Gone for at least forty-five minutes. I had even encouraged her to go as a Mother's Day treat. Our eldest child, two at the time, was preoccupied with Elmo on the television. The youngest had been down in her crib for a nap. It would be long enough for me to sneak away to our home office, shut the door, and get on the computer. But what I didn't know was the salon was closed for Mother's Day, and as Paul Harvey used to say, "Now you know the rest of the story." Jen had found me out. She felt betrayed and devastated, and I felt exposed, ashamed, helpless, hopeless, and weak.

At that point in my life, my source of pornography was *always* the computer. After all, the Internet makes it easy. Anything and everything you could want is there. Want to know the latest news? Need a quick recipe to make for company? Craving for the latest celebrity gossip? No problem! Real, fake, truth, falsehood, it is all there. All you have to do is just open up Google and search for it. And search for porn I did.

With pornography, the first thing to realize is that we all have a choice. We can choose God or we can choose the sin. We can choose to be either obedient or disobedient. Sounds simple. Why then is it so hard to choose God? What drives us to choose sin again and again?

Frustrated and oppressed by my guilt, I desperately prayed to God, calling out and asking Him, "Why can't I beat this? Why do I keep failing?"

I heard nothing.

So, I asked, time and time again, pleading with Him, "Why am I so burdened with this? I've struggled with this for so long! Why won't you just take it all away?"

Again, multiple times, no answer.

Hurt and discouraged by God's lack of response, I finally decided to sit there and wait. I sat in silence waiting anxiously, hoping the clouds would part and God would finally give me an answer. It was only a few minutes, but it seemed much longer. Then, my mind began to let go of my anxiety. My body and spirit began to become calm, and then, God gently spoke. The simplicity of His response hit me.

"Craig, you are trying to fill a space that only I can fill."

This perfectly summed up my reasons for failure. I was trying to replace God with my own inadequate inventions. I was trying to substitute something made by man for something that God had already created. No wonder I was failing!

Now that I knew *why* I was failing, how was I supposed to stop? Well, if it were really easy, then I wouldn't be writing this book and you wouldn't be reading it. The truth is it's *really* hard. It's very hard to choose God over sin. Paul said, "I don't really understand myself, for I want to do what is right, but I don't do it. Instead, I do what I hate" (Romans 7:15).

One of the most frustrating aspects of the pornography addiction is its cyclical nature. Have you ever experienced something like this? You go a little while without looking at porn and start to feel good about yourself. You might even think, *I've finally beaten it!* Then, out of the blue, something happens. You hear bad news from a friend or family member. You begin experiencing increased stress at work or home. You start to feel stagnant in your personal or professional life. Then you start looking for an outlet for your stress or emotions. And that's when you fall.

Part of this has to do with our sinful nature. We will always struggle with our flesh. But along this journey, I've discovered four delusions that trap us in the cycle of pornography addiction. I've experienced all four. Some of this may apply to you, and some may not. What's important is to recognize them for what they are—*delusions.*

Here's the bad news: we have allowed ourselves to be duped, distracted, and diverted from what truly satisfies. Once we admit that we have been deluded by the dark world of pornography, we can begin to accept that we cannot live under the oppression of falsehood. When we finally proclaim that we are tired of the sneaking around in the dark—when we admit to lying to ourselves and to those we love—we can then turn our attention to the good news. And the good news is this: *Truth shatters delusions.*

DELUSION #1: Once I get married, I won't need pornography.

This was the hardest for me to accept. I dated a lot before I met Jen, and sadly, some of these relationships involved sex.

Regardless, I still continued to view pornography throughout my relationships. This frustrated me, because I thought at the time that pornography was driven by my desire to have sex. As a result, I rationalized that the infrequent nature of sex in these relationships wasn't enough to satisfy my carnal urges.

When I met Jen and we got serious right away, I convinced myself that I wouldn't need pornography after we were married. After all, I could have sex anytime I wanted, right? Well, those of you who are addicted to porn and are married already know the answer. The addiction doesn't stop after marriage. The main reason it doesn't is because pornography is not about sex. Okay, pick your jaw up off the floor. You read correctly. It's not about sex! It's the *illusion* of sex. It's about fantasy. And it's about control—the control of your imagination and your mind. In truth though, fantasy never measures up to reality.

When you use porn, you're participating via your mind. That's what makes it so dangerous, and that's why it doesn't stop after marriage. Your mind doesn't change when you get married, and even if you are having sex on a regular basis, that alone will not end your desire to watch pornography.

Some of you may have involved your wives in your addiction. You might watch porn together or perhaps you have made your own porn. If that describes you, I strongly urge you and your spouse to end that practice. The act of sex was created by God to be shared with you and your wife, no one else. By watching pornography together to "get in the mood," you are seeking inspiration outside of God. As if that isn't bad enough, the joint participation brings up a couple of other issues.

First, it sends mixed signals to the man. It tells him that porn is okay. This means he will feel less inclined to abstain from watching it when his wife is not around. Second, the use of pornography in marriage creates a false intimacy. After all, porn is about creating a fantasy. It's about the delivery guy, the pool guy, the college chick in a plaid skirt, and many, many other darker scenarios. None of these are what God intended sex to be. Sex is designed to be a holy act between a husband and his wife. God created it to be pure, as the symbolic union of Christ and the church. He has called us to be pure as well.

DELUSION #2: Internet filters can curb, and maybe cure, my addiction.

After the first time Jen had caught me, we talked about setting filters on the computer. We looked at several different types of software but settled on using the parental controls included with the computer's operating system. This didn't work for us, mainly because I'm the more technically inclined one and I found a way around the filter. The parental controls included with a computer's operating system are not very robust.

Perhaps you have experienced success with filtering software. In my experience, setting up software safeguards is only a temporary fix. It's merely a defensive wall, and walls can be compromised. The problem of pornography runs deeper, and so the solution to the addiction must be even deeper than that.

When I was in high school, a burglar broke into a neighbor's house. I discussed the incident with my dad and suggested we get an alarm system for our own home. Dad agreed that we should take smart precautions such as locking doors and windows, but what he said next stuck with me. "Craig, if someone really wants to break into your home, they are going to do it. And all of your preparation won't be able to stop them."

Even if you have Internet filters or filtering software on your computer, it doesn't mean you can't find pornography. Pornography appears "offline" in magazines, digital media (i.e., DVDs, Blu-rays), and on cable and satellite TV. Movie channels often have "soft core" pornography as part of the "after dark" programming. Increasingly, cable providers also grant access to their "on demand" libraries that contain many of the same movies. Streaming services online also carry "soft core" pornography as part of their libraries. Smart phones and tablets have Internet browsers and porn applications, not all of which are caught by the rating system. There is no shortage of access to porn.

In addition to the explicit images, there are many suggestive images out there as well. Internet ads are everywhere. In my e-mail, I'm often presented with advertisements for single women looking for "love." If you do any sort of browsing around the Internet— and nearly everyone does—you've seen similar ads. Couple these with the assortment of sexually suggestive print advertisements, TV commercials, and even radio ads, and it's no wonder we feel constantly tempted!

If you're the spouse looking for ways to guard your family from the availability of porn, the task may seem insurmountable. Pornography and the temptation to find it are everywhere.

After I experienced relapse after relapse, Jen ultimately came to the conclusion that she couldn't possibly hope to keep me from it. Even the thought of trying to do so was too exhausting. As she described how tired she was from worrying about it, I pictured her in front of the proverbial leaking dam. No matter how hard she tried, no matter how much she wanted to, she couldn't keep me from every temptation. Jen finally realized that if she wanted to help me out of my addiction to porn, we had to attack the reason for the addiction, not the temptations themselves.

DELUSION #3: Pornography makes me feel like a man without actually having to be one.

As men, we want respect. I would go so far as to say that we actually need it. It feels affirming to be wanted and to be seen as desirable. Sex between a husband and a wife can be the ultimate display and fulfillment of this desire. The producers of pornography understand this basic need/desire of men, but in their hands it is twisted into something much darker.

The situations in pornographic videos and magazines show ready and available women. They depict women who crave men or, in some cases, other women. This is designed to prey upon the strong desire of each man to be wanted. It also preys upon the strong desire of a woman to feel beautiful and wanted. But with pornography it's not about freedom; it's about control. It's not about respect, but rather domination. It's a dark false reality.

Human beings are *obsessed* with appearances. But like the costumes and make-up of a play, it's fake. Porn tries to convince us that it's real. The world tells us that we have to be sexy—and then redefines what is supposed to be pure love into a mere photo-enhanced falsehood.

If we listen to the world, we have to have the "perfect" body, but that body is at best elusive and at worst unattainable. We yearn to be attractive, but beauty is relative and temporary. We long to be desirable, but the love and affections of other people are fickle and insufficient. The truth is that it's not about our bodies. It's not about being beautiful or getting everyone to want us. It's about loving God and loving our spouse as ourselves.

Once we realize that it's not real, we begin to understand the true nature of what we were watching: brokenness. The actors and actresses that are participating in these movies are broken people. I didn't really bother to ask myself who these actors and actresses were while I was in the midst of my addiction. It didn't occur to me that they might be victims themselves, that they might not really enjoy what they are doing and might not love themselves. It didn't occur to me that they are deeply dissatisfied people looking for fulfillment. All I cared about was what I could get out of it.

Through the process of working through my addiction and doing research for this book, I began to learn about the realities of the porn industry. It's very different than what I observed on the screen. There are now organizations out there helping to shed light on the porn industry (e.g., www.fightthenewdrug.org). It's essential for those who are struggling with porn to understand what they are actually watching and supporting.

The other draw of pornography is a false sense of acceptance. In the fantasy world, you can be whoever you want to be. When you place yourself into the dream, you don't feel the pain of rejection. You don't experience the sense of inadequacy. You don't see yourself for who you are. You see yourself for what you want. But like the videos or images you are viewing, it isn't real. If you want to be free, truly free, it starts by accepting the truth. And the truth is this: God created you in His image! (See Genesis 1:26–27.) He accepts you, and He loves you. You are worth far more than any fleeting fantasy.

DELUSION #4: There's no way out—I'll never be free.

Go to any bookstore and take a gander at the self-help section. It's rife with tomes of how to improve every aspect of your life. Feeling anxious? Want to be more assertive? Are you depressed? There's a book for that.

Throughout my addiction, I have often gone to God for help. However, I have been so wrapped up in myself that I failed to listen to what He was trying to tell me. I cried out a lot but very rarely was I quiet enough to listen for His voice.

My addiction was a vicious cycle. I'd sin, feel guilty, repent, feel better. I never seemed able to overcome my addiction. As a result, I went through periods of hot and cold relationships with God. I'd go to a conference, go on a mission trip, or maybe just get more diligent with my quiet times. These might get me on fire for God for a few days, maybe even a few weeks, but like the seeds in the parable of the sower[1] that fell along the briars, my fruit never developed. I never seemed to tend my garden well. As a result, my fruit suffered, as did I.

On that Mother's Day, a serious break occurred. I thought my transgression would mean the end of my marriage. My mind went wild with my ominous new future. Gone would be my wife of seven years and my two girls. How could Jen stay with me? I pictured her leaving, taking the girls with her, and I would never see them again. In my state of mind, I wasn't even sure that I deserved to have them anymore. In this new future that I pictured, I'd be alone. That image terrified me. I became angry with myself for my weakness, and I had no clue what to do about it.

I thought, *I can't beat this. I give up.* I felt so hopeless. On top of that I felt a tremendous amount of guilt. Not only did I have the guilt of committing one sin weighing down on me, I also had the guilt associated with the countless lies I had told and the deceit I used with Jen. It's easy to understand some of what I was feeling. After all, no one likes hearing that they've made a mistake, especially when that mistake causes someone you love extreme pain. But this feeling of inadequacy was more than that. I didn't just feel like a failure to her and myself. I believed I was a fraud and didn't deserve Jen. And I was scared she was starting to feel that way too.

Yet not even the seriousness of what took place that Mother's Day was enough to keep me from looking at porn. It took another five years to truly come to terms with what would end this cycle. Even though God had told me I was using porn to fill a space that only He was designed to fill, I didn't really believe Him. I didn't really trust Him.

Through a long process of relationship-building and the prayers of those who love me, I have become living proof that we can be free from porn addiction. *The cycle-breaker is a true and intimate relationship with Jesus.* His love and guidance keep me from seeking fulfillment and release from pornography. He is the only real answer to our problem. Who better to know you than the One who created you? Paul talks about this relationship in Colossians 1:15–20.

> Christ is the visible image of the invisible God. He existed before anything was created and is supreme over all creation, for through him God created everything in the heavenly realms and on earth. He made the things we can see and the things we can't see—such as thrones, kingdoms, rulers, and authorities in the unseen world. Everything was created through him and for him. He existed before anything else, and he holds all creation together. Christ is also the head of the church, which is his body. He is the beginning, supreme over all who rise from the dead. So he is first in everything. For God in all his fullness was pleased to live in Christ, and through him God reconciled everything to himself. He made peace with

everything in heaven and on earth by means of Christ's blood on the cross.

So God created everything through Jesus and for Jesus. That includes you and me. God has reconciled us all to him through the power of the cross. You have access to that same forgiveness and love of God. All you have to do is claim it. Jesus will respond. I promise you.

Paul goes on to say in Colossians 1:

This includes you who were once far away from God. You were his enemies, separated from him by your evil thoughts and actions. Yet now he has reconciled you to himself through the death of Christ in his physical body. As a result, he has brought you into his own presence, and you are holy and blameless as you stand before him without a single fault.

But you must continue to believe this truth and stand firmly in it. Don't drift away from the assurance you received when you heard the Good News. The Good News has been preached all over the world, and I, Paul, have been appointed as God's servant to proclaim it. (vv. 21–23)

Today, I'm a recovering porn addict and actively cultivating a relationship with Jesus. Only He can fill the void that I have been trying to fill for most of my life. You have this same void, the same God-shaped hole. We all try different things: money, fame, sex, drugs, whatever we can. But it's a unique shape that only God can fill.

If you are trying to beat this addiction with willpower alone, you are going to fail! It's not about willpower. It's about a relationship—your relationship with God and His Son Jesus. The power of temptation is strong but we serve a God who is stronger.

I have no idea where you are in your walk with Jesus. But without Him, there is no victory. You will struggle with this battle all of your life and it will cost you dearly. You will not win. That's the bad news. The good news is that we serve a mighty God and He's already won the war.

CHAPTER 6

Building a Foundation of Truth

As the Scriptures say, "A man leaves his father and mother and is joined to his wife, and the two are united into one." This is a great mystery, but it is an illustration of the way Christ and the church are one.

Ephesians 5:31–32

After the priest (who happened to be my future father-in-law) asked Craig if he would have me be to be his wife, to live with me in the covenant of marriage, loving me, comforting, honoring, and keeping me in sickness and in health, forsaking all others and being faithful as long as we both shall live, Craig didn't give the customary response, "I will." No, he said, "You bet I will!" The whole congregation laughed and rejoiced with me that I had found someone who clearly desired to love me and love me with so much conviction.

I'm sure my father greatly appreciated Craig's added enthusiasm before he had to release my hand and give me over to my soon-to-be husband. On the surface, it looked like everything was going to be great. We had met at church. We both were raised in the same denomination. We understood that we were leaving our existing families and entering in a covenant relationship before God that was both spiritually and legally binding. We knew something about sex being part of the process of uniting the two of us into one (although I'm sure my dad did not want to think about *that*). Oh, and of course we had done some pre-marital counseling. We were good to go.

Clearly, we were not as good to go as we thought we were. At the ripe age of twenty-two, I knew only vaguely what the Bible said about sex, submission, love, and the roles of husband of wife. I started tuning out at the mere mention of the word "submit" in Paul's letter to the Ephesians. What kind of wife *submits* to her husband? One with no backbone? We weren't in the 1950s anymore. Surely, God did not mean I would have to do that in this day and age.

We've talked in chapters 4 and 5 about the illusions and delusions we face when grappling with pornography. But what about those illusions and delusions we have about marriage? I was deluding myself that God's Word isn't meant for *my* marriage, just as much as Craig was deluding himself that his porn addiction would go away because he would be able to have sex with me. And we both suffered from the illusion that our marriage would be smooth sailing. *All* marriages take work; *all* marriages go through rough patches.

Perhaps you feel as though your marriage is broken, shattered into a million pieces. And that might be a very true picture. But God is amazing at putting things back together. What if we laid down our ideas about what we thought marriage *should* be and let God rebuild it according to His specifications? If it's already in shambles, what else do we have to lose? Nothing. What do we have to gain by building on His foundation of truth? Everything.

What Happens on the Wedding Day?

Why don't we go back to the beginning? What are God's intentions for the wedding day? In most marriages we make a choice to come together to wed, to be joined in marriage with another person. This means that we leave our mother and father to start a new family. This is part of the process that God laid out for us. Jesus says, "This explains why a man leaves his father and mother and is joined to his wife, and the two are united into one" (Matthew 19:5).

In this passage, the Greek word for "joined" is *kollaō*, which means to "unite" or "cling to." Essentially, this verse refers to the purpose for which a man and a woman choose to leave their parents. But Jesus' words about marriage do not stop there. He continues: "Since they are no longer two but one, let no one split apart what God has joined together" (Matthew 19:6).

There is a supernatural occurrence when we marry before God. We may *choose* to join, but *God does the actual joining.* To highlight this point, Jesus continues by saying that what God brings together, human beings have no business tearing apart. It has ceased to just be about the decision two people make to come together. No longer is it just about you. It's about God, too.

When you say your vows, you make promises to each other in front of God to love each other forever. Even when the passion dies down. Even when arguments happen. Even when your interests diverge. Even when your spouse sins against you. You are committed to this relationship and you sign this covenant on the wedding night by consummating the marriage (i.e., you have sex). Therefore, each time you have sex, you are reminded of your vows. You remember that you are in this for the long haul. And you remember that you took these vows in front of God and that it was the power of God that brought you together. And He doesn't want any part of this world to bring separation to His union.

This may be why Jesus chooses two different words for "joined" in Matthew 19:5 and 19:6. In verse 5 he uses *kollaō,* a word that helps us see that the purpose of our leaving is to be joined. In verse 6 he uses the word *syzeugnymi*, which means "to yoke" or "fasten together." What do you think about when you hear the word "yoked"? I think of oxen, strapped together and hemmed in to work as a team and accomplish a common goal. The two oxen have been bound together as one entity by the person who has trained them for their work. The word *syzeugnymi* reinforces the fact that couples have been strapped together by God himself.

We are reined in, bound by God's Word—His directions for how to love and cherish and ultimately do the work He has asked us to do. He doesn't expect us to live up to this covenant by ourselves. A rancher doesn't expect the oxen to wake up, strap themselves to the plow, and head out to the fields on their own. God doesn't expect us to keep a marriage together based solely on our abilities and willpower. He is fully prepared to be a part of our marriage if we will allow Him to be. God never gives us a task that He expects us to do by ourselves. Remember, He promises that He will be with us always.

Marriage Is Not Just about Us

What if this means that when we are married we are to work together to accomplish a God-given goal, with God's help? What if this means that if we want to experience the full fruits of marriage, we need to involve God and His power beyond the wedding day? What if it is more than just taking care of each other and loving each other? What if it's less about *us* and more about *Jesus*?

Skip Moen, dean of the Department of Biblical Leadership at Master's International Divinity School, says this:

Two people who are joined together in an agreement for mutual pleasure, protection and provision are not necessarily yoked. To be yoked is to share the same task. This is the purpose of marriage as God sees it. My spouse and I must share in the same God-given objective. Without this, we are joined but not yoked. Of course, that doesn't mean we do the same job. We may both have different tasks but we have the same objective. What is that? It is to live in yoked harmony, recapturing what it means to be one again in a display of *perfect redemption*.[1]

When I think about the words "perfect redemption," I automatically think about what Jesus did on the cross for me and for you. I think of the sacrifice He made so that I would be spared from eternal separation from God. I think about how His act communicates forgiveness, unconditional love, and deliverance from all that entangles me in this world. And then I read these words:

"A man leaves his father and mother and is joined to his wife, and the two are united into one." This is a great mystery, but it is an illustration of the way Christ and the church are one. (Ephesians 5:31–32)

Could it be possible that God created marriage to be a tangible example of how Christ views the church? And by the church, I don't mean the building, I mean *us*—the body of people who follow Christ. Could it be that God's primary purpose for marriage is not happiness or companionship, but so "you and your spouse can be a living, breathing, physical picture to the world of Jesus and His Bride [the church]?"[2] It seems like a tall order. How can we ever live up to such a task, especially when our relationship has been marred by pornography use?

How Do We Work Together?

This is the great thing about God. He is not ambiguous. We may not understand everything about Him, but He gave us an entire book on how to follow Him in our lives. Our marriages are no exception, especially since they are intended to depict how He desires us to see Him in relationship to His people. He knows this will not be easy. He knows we continually live out of our own selfishness, worry, and fears. And yet He still thinks we can do this—with His help, of course.

The passage of Scripture that we are going to study next is filled with debate. In my research I read articles that conflicted, even though both writers had a lot of letters after their names. Much of the debate centers on the word "submit." Even today, I have a hard time moving past the societal connotations and cultural influence that revolve around this world. To help us get in tune with how God wants us to understand and internalize this word, I recommend that we stop and pray. In the book of James, he writes if any one of us lacks wisdom, all we need to do is ask and the Father will gladly oblige (James 1:5). Let's ask God for His wisdom (which so often greatly differs from the world's) before we continue. Would you pray this prayer with us?

Father God, you know the spirit of which you penned these words through your servants. You have called each of us to live them out in our lives. You know our specific situations, and yet you still wrote these words to apply to everyone. Show us how to apply them in our marriage. Give us your wisdom and help us interpret them always in the spirit of your love. Amen.

Let's look together at one portion of God's guidelines for marriage in Ephesians 5:21–30 as written in the New Living Translation. We will break it down section by section and see how it directly applies to our own marriages and how God's Word defines who we are as a couple and what roles we play within our union. The discussion questions are placed at the end of each section of verses instead of at the end of the chapter for ease of reference to the Scripture.

"And further, submit to one another out of reverence for Christ" (v. 21).

The Greek word for "submit" in this verse does mean to "put in subjection," but it also means to "submit one's control." In fact, the term was a Greek military term that came to be used in non-military situations to mean having a "voluntary attitude of giving in, cooperating, assuming responsibility, and carrying a burden."[3]

Think about the yoked oxen. If you are truly a team, tethered to Christ, working for His greater purposes, there has to be a relinquishment of control, both to each other and to Christ, in order for the work to be done. You are working together as one; therefore, if one of you stops carrying part of the load that Christ has given to you, what does that do to your partner? If one of you becomes uncooperative with God's will, what do you imagine happens to your team? If we cannot yield control to Him, we cannot love and respect Him in the way that He has called us to.

When I visualize what this verse communicates to us as a married couple, I picture us kneeling together holding hands, bowing together to Christ. It is a communal act that shows that we have Christ as our head and that we both wish to serve Him out of love. We will still have our individual relationships with Christ. We will each have our different areas of service, but we will always be working together to bring glory to Jesus.

For you to discuss together:

1. Do you think that God has a greater purpose for your marriage than just your own happiness? What do you think about your marriage not just being about you?

2. Would you be willing to spend time talking and praying about how God is calling you to work together for Him? List your strengths as individuals and as a couple.

3. Take turns describing what your individual relationships with Christ look like. What areas do you see God working in your life? What areas would you like to invite Him to change?

4. In what ways could you work to make your relationship as a couple Christ-centered? How has porn detracted from your individual relationship with Jesus? How has it affected your ability to work as a team?

"For wives, this means submit to your husbands as to the Lord. For a husband is the head of his wife as Christ is the head of the church. He is the Savior of his body, the church. As the church submits to Christ, so you wives should submit to your husbands in everything" (vv. 22–24).

Ultimately, Christ has us tethered to Him and He is leading us to do the work He has called us to do. Both husband and wife are accountable to God in their individual relationships with Him. Here is where the Word can get hard to swallow, especially when the wife has been hurt by porn addiction.

As wives, we are called to submit to our husbands. The Greek root word used for the word submit is *hypotassō*, and it means that as wives, we are to do things such as *obey, submit one's self,* and *to yield to one's advice.* Before you let all sorts of walls go up around your heart and name all sorts of reasons why your spouse is not worthy of your submission, I would like to you pause right here. Take a deep breath and think for a moment about whether or not you trust God.

This passage is not asking you to accept your spouse's porn use. It is not asking you to be a doormat or to tolerate abuse. It is not asking you to relegate yourself to a corner and never utter your opinion or your perspective. (And if you *are* in an abusive situation—physically, sexually, verbally, or emotionally, you need help different than what the scope of this book can provide. Please see appendix A for help.)

God intended husbands to lead. Many of them do not understand how to do this in the way that God intended. However, this does not mean that wives can stop giving their husbands respect and authority in our lives.

Because I was so hurt by Craig's porn use and because I knew it was not what God intended for Him, I made the mistake of assuming that Craig was incapable of leading in any part of our marriage and did not deserve my respect. By making these assumptions about his sin and treating him with *dis*respect, I became just as much a sinner in our relationship.

Think about this: If the wife assumes the husband cannot do anything, what is the husband's motivation to change? If the wife assumes all responsibility, where does a husband have space to grow into his God-given responsibility? Porn use is an indicator of a hurting heart. Hurting hearts need to be built up, not torn down.

For you to discuss together:

1. Wives, what are your fears about submitting to your husband? Husbands, what are your fears about leading your household?

2. Where do you see the husband already leading? What are the leadership strengths that the husband possesses? What does he do well?

3. Wives, are there any responsibilities you feel you have, but shouldn't have? Are you willing to start turning them over?

4. Husbands, what can your wife do to show you respect? Wives, what can you do today to show your husband that you respect him?

5. Husbands, what can you do to garner respect?

"For husbands, this means love your wives, just as Christ loved the church. He gave up his life for her to make her holy and clean, washed by the cleansing of God's word. He did this to present her to himself as a glorious church without a spot or wrinkle or any other blemish. Instead, she will be holy and without fault. In the same way, husbands ought to love their wives as they love their own bodies. For a man who loves his wife actually shows love for himself. No one hates his own body but feeds and cares for it, just as Christ cares for the church. And we are members of his body" (vv. 25–30).

The word for "love" in this passage is a form of the Greek word *agape*. Before the New Testament was written, this version of the word love was rarely used, perhaps because the life of Jesus was necessary to bring it to life and for us to understand its true meaning by looking at His example for us. The other Greek words for love are *eraō* (which means sexual passion), *storgeō* (family devotion), and *phileō* (friendship).

Paul, the author of Ephesians, chooses the word *agapaō* to show husbands how they are intended to love their wives. The love wives should receive from their husbands is meant to be a living, breathing example of how Christ loves us, His church. *Agape* love is self-sacrificing, filled with compassion, kindness, and generosity. John, a disciple of Jesus and the author of one of the four gospels in the New Testament, uses the word *agape* to describe the very essence of God.[4]

Jesus sacrificed himself so that we could have unity with God. He provided a way for us to be free from our sin so that nothing could separate us from His Father. After Jesus, we no longer had to participate in ritual sacrifices or jump through ornate hoops to bring ourselves back into relationship with God. Rather, Jesus paved the way for us to simply come before God and ask for forgiveness. Through this sacrifice and grace, Jesus and the church live in unity.

When a husband loves his wife in a sacrificial way—when he seeks to meet her needs generously and with kindness—he is actually showing love to himself as well. Think for a moment: When you make someone else happy, when you do something or give something, it affects you too. And often, you receive something back. When the husband chooses to actively love his wife, he is loving himself as well, not only because they have been joined together by God but because his wife will often return his love with respect.

It is this cycle that often gets interrupted by many things in this world, but especially by porn use. Husbands must realize that by engaging in pornography they are choosing not to love their wives. Not only are they neglecting the *loving*, they are contaminating the very act that serves as a reminder of the vows they took on their wedding day.

Pornography is a crutch. To love your wife sacrificially is to give up the crutch. Earlier we asked your wife if she could trust God. This is the time to ask yourself the same question. Can you trust God enough to ask Him to help you remove the crutch and stand firm in Him?

For you to discuss together:

1. Wives, what makes you feel loved? Husbands, what do you do to show your wife love? Do these answers match up? If not, what could you change to make sure he or she feels loved?

2. What can you do to be more loveable?

3. What does sacrificial love look like within the context of your relationship?

4. Do you believe that if your spouse feels loved you will reap the benefits? How might this play out?

5. How was love shown in your respective upbringings? Is this something you want to repeat or change? Why?

Love, Respect, and Sex

Satan uses porn to drive a wedge between you and your spouse. He actively tries to separate what God has joined together, especially since marriage is supposed to bear witness to Christ and the relationship He has to the church. But just because porn has torn at the very fabric of your marriage does not mean that God cannot stitch you back together in a way where sex regains its pure purpose. Through deliberate dependence on Him, you will learn how He can heal your marriage and allow you to function and love your roles as husbands and wives. It will take time, discussion, and dedication to build your marriage on the foundation of biblical truth. But remember, He never asks you to go at it alone.

PART 3

Letting Go and Letting God

CHAPTER 7

Surrender

I cried out, "I am slipping!"
but your unfailing love, O LORD,
supported me.
When doubts filled my mind,
your comfort gave me renewed hope
and cheer.

Psalm 94:18–19

■ Her

Confession time: I wasn't the only one plotting and scheming in regards to porn. No, I wasn't rearranging my life so that I could watch it. I was rearranging my life so I could catch Craig while *he* was watching it.

Before that Mother's Day when I shut myself in the closet and railed at God for the wretched problem He had let infiltrate my life, I shouldered much of the responsibility for keeping Craig away from porn. Mix intense anger with a naturally controlling personality and you've got a recipe for disaster.

I told you in chapter 1 about some of the stopgaps that we put in place to help keep Craig away from porn. These protective measures, such as leaving the study door open, facing the computer screen toward the door, and using filtering software, are good things to do. However, I didn't realize the way that I enforced these rules was not conducive to creating an environment where Craig wanted to follow them.

For example, if the door to the study was closed, I would quickly burst in, demand to know why the door was closed, and then chastise him for breaking the rule. Other times, if I was upstairs and he was downstairs at night, I would quietly creep down the stairs, hoping my presence would be unknown until I could see what images lit up his computer screen. My behaviors had become steeped in just as much secrecy and scheming as his.

Some nights I would wake up in the early morning hours and find he was missing from our bed. I would immediately get up, my entire body trembling, my stomach in one huge knot. Fear and dread would pulsate in my body from head to toe. I would set out to find him, armed with this fear and anger. Even if he wasn't looking at porn, I would still be upset that I had to get out of bed to check up on him. After that much adrenaline floods my body, sleep is a far-off dream. If I am really honest, there were times that I wanted to catch him looking at porn so that I would have the opportunity to rightfully (in my mind) unleash my fury. And it wouldn't just be my fury from this incident, but from all those past as well.

I don't know about your situation, but my husband has a bit of a rebellious streak in him. Even when I was reminding him of mutually established parameters and goals we devised, he would become huffy and continue on with behaviors that could easily lead down a destructive path. He saw the rules as something designed to constrain him, thus, he would look for ways to break free from what he viewed as my tight grasp of his behavior. As such, he would engage in behaviors he knew would hurt me deeply. He would spend hours playing video games. He would neglect to help me around the house. He wouldn't talk to me about anything of real substance. Trying to keep him accountable at this stage had no positive returns.

I would take this rebellion as his inability or unwillingness to fight for our marriage. He would take this as my inability to see him for anything other than a porn addict. The rules we had set up to create a pathway to freedom ended up becoming a locked-down prison. The padlock was fear; the key was surrender.

I caught my first glimmer of this key on the floor of my bathroom closet on that Mother's Day. I felt as though I had no choice but to grab hold of it. Everything that I had done to try to save my husband only seemed to make matters worse.

When I look back at myself that day, a crumpled heap on the floor, I can see clearly that every single one of the rules we had implemented was rooted in fear. My sneaking and scheming to try to catch him in the act was motivated by fear. My threatening and chastising was instigated by fear. I had been like a military dictator that wanted precise order and regulation because, like most dictators, I was afraid that something or someone more powerful than me would take over. I feared that porn would completely and totally take over and rule our lives.

That soul-crushing moment on Mother's Day led me to realize that I could no longer carry the weight of Craig's porn addiction on my shoulders. I left his addiction on the bathroom floor, but it wasn't easy to keep from grasping it again and hoisting it back on my shoulders. I had to let God train me how to leave it there, at the foot of the cross, in His hands, or however else you could imagine it. *He had to teach me that giving up control was not the same as giving in to porn.*

Harnessing the Fear

When I first realized the extent of Craig's addiction, it terrified me. All I wanted to do was to make it stop. Clearly, this is not a bad desire. What I had to realize, however, is that God seeks lasting change. He seeks relationship. He seeks to turn everything that Satan means for harm into good.[1] All of these things require a process. They all require time. And thus, my "hurry-up-already" perspective was not in line with God's. His way is the best way and therefore, I had to get out of the way.

My fear skewed my perspective of the process God was leading Craig through. Here I will highlight some of my main fears and show how God transformed my perspective into one where I saw Him as always in control. Once I acknowledged my own fears and allowed God to work in *my* heart, I was able to leave Craig in God's hands.

Fear #1: *If he gives into temptation, he'll be back to square one.* God again used my food addiction to help me overcome this fear. If I had a bad day and used food for comfort, eating way too much and for the wrong reasons, I wouldn't automatically regain everything I had lost, mentally or physically. I could come back to God, dust the crumbs off my mouth, and ask for forgiveness. Through repentance and introspection, God could help me discover why I had slipped, thus fortifying me against the next temptation. So often with addictions, as we will discover in a later chapter, there are layers upon layers of hurts, false reasons, and sins that must be uncovered before long-lasting change can occur. I needed to have faith that God would use each slip for good, to uncover something else in Craig's heart, and to further prove to Craig that no matter what the sin, He will always be there to welcome him home.

Fear #2: *If I don't pester him, he'll forget that this is really bad for him.* Most husbands—indeed, most people—are built with a natural aversion to nagging. There is a difference between me asking Craig about his struggle with pornography and constantly following him around, looking over his shoulder to make sure he's being appropriate. Not only does this make him feel like a child, it is also emotionally and physically exhausting for me. I already have two children who need my ever-watchful eye, and God has created me for the job to watch over them and protect *them*. In my relationship with Craig, I was more concerned about him following the rules than I was about his relationship with Jesus. Thus, it wasn't clear to Craig that I really cared about him and the ordeal he was going through. He just thought I wanted the porn gone.

Fear #3: *If we don't nip this in the bud now, it could escalate.* The truth is, it can. The statistics show it. But this wasn't my reality then. It is easy to go down the road where you predict all the bad things that could possibly happen. But what kept this fear at bay after my surrender was the truth that God can redeem all things. There is no situation bigger than Him. There is nothing He does not forgive, so there is nothing I cannot forgive with God's grace and guidance. To fear the future was to steal any joy that I found in the present.

Satan used my fears to keep Craig entrapped in so many ways when I thought they would help keep him safe. He used my fears to entrap me, to make me a slave to control and power. But God asks us to fear Him out of respect and obedience, not to become a slave to control. Part of fearing God alone is recognizing that He can handle *all* things. Fearing things that people *could* do simply takes focus off my own relationship with Jesus and does nothing to move my husband closer to his Savior.

Speaking with Love and Respect

Here's the thing: I can be a bit demanding, especially when I'm afraid. I want people to just do what I want them to do so I can feel in control, safe, and generally okay. In many ways, I had made Craig's porn addiction about me—fearing what was happening to me and what *could* happen to me. Often, I would go into self-protection mode, which again was fear-based. When I allowed God to harness my fear, there was so much more space for me to be loving and respectful because I was no longer focused on myself and how his porn use affected my world.

Allowing love and respect to be my primary motivation led to a radical change in the tone of my voice and the words I spoke. Instead of telling Craig what to do, I could ask him what he thought. Instead of instituting a new plan of attack, I could ask him what he believed he needed for success. I could step back and find the ways he receives love so he knew I was actually seeing *him* again, not just his porn addiction.

Craig has told me many times that talking about his porn addiction is fruitful. It keeps him cognizant of the fact that this is (and may always be) a daily battle. Having conversations that linked his progress and his budding relationship with Jesus helped keep hope in the forefront for both of us. The conversation had to focus on hope and light or else it would be lumped into the category of nagging.

Craig and I still sometimes have differing opinions about what is okay for him to watch. A recent topic of discussion centered on the HBO series *Game of Thrones*. At the time, we didn't have cable, but his friends did, so they invited him to watch with them. To me, anything with nudity should be off-limits, but ultimately, it's not my choice. And so I simply said, "Craig, I get worried that shows like this could send you down a path that leads to temptation and acts that you know you don't want to do. Would you consider praying about watching this show before you go?"

I stated my opinion but in a way that invited further relationship with Jesus for both of us. I acknowledged that I have worry and fear that I needed to take to Jesus, while asking Craig to honor Jesus and me by seeking the Lord with this request. I didn't enforce my will or make him feel bad for considering the choice to watch the show. I've shown him I trust that he will seek God, and I've stepped back, leaving him in God's hands.

The Power of Prayer

Since that first day of surrender, I have found solace in prayer more than anything else. When the physical sensation of fear arises, I stop first to pray before I do anything. I simply ask God, "Is there something I should do in this moment?" More often than not, He prompts me to pray for Craig—for protection, strength, and guidance. I pray that Jesus would show up in tangible ways in Craig's life. I pray that if at any point I am to intervene, God would make it abundantly clear. And I pray that if I am not supposed to do or say anything, God would keep me rooted in His peace.

During a particularly hard time for Craig, I asked God to wake me up if Craig was being lured out of bed by temptation. On several occasions, God has done this. The one incident that sticks in my mind happened not long after that Mother's Day. First, let me say I fully believe God woke me up. At the time, we had a two-year-old who didn't sleep well and a baby who still needed to eat during the night. Anytime I was actually sleeping, I was out, undisturbed by Craig's movements in the night.

As Craig stood up to leave the room, I awoke and asked him where he was going, knowing full well that his leaving was not indicative of anything positive. He told me (at about 2:00 a.m.) that he remembered he had work to do. He was barely coherent and he didn't seem like he was fully himself. I was able to lovingly persuade him that his "work" could wait and got him back to sleep, my arms wrapped around him.

The next morning, I asked him if he remembered the incident. He did, and amazingly, he also admitted that he was going to pursue the temptation in those early morning hours. I told him I had specifically prayed for the opportunity to intervene if temptation arose in the middle of the night and that I was so proud of him for coming back to bed.

This incident is proof that God can take an unpleasant situation and reveal goodness. First, He affirmed for me that He hears and answers prayer. I went to God and asked Him to help keep Craig safe and enable me to participate as needed. This incident was an incredible confidence builder for me in my own walk with God.

Second, He showed Craig accountability can work between husband and wife in regard to porn addiction. A wife, prompted by God, can provide a way out for the husband from the clutch of temptation. Craig saw that I acted in response to God's work and urging. Therefore, my words and actions looked different than all those in the past, where I acted out of my own fear and anger. My tone had changed. My physical demeanor changed. My response to his temptation changed. Instead of freaking out, I enveloped him. Instead of judging him, I forgave him. Instead of using more rules, I thanked God for using me.

Stormie Omartian writes in her book *The Power of a Praying Wife*, "One of the greatest gifts you can give your husband is your wholeness. The most effective tool in transforming him may be your own transformation."[2]

I had to let God work on my own mess so I could effectively help my husband in the way that God intended me to help him. There was just as much I needed to surrender as Craig did. As we both began to give way to God's presence in our lives and trust Him more intimately and more thoroughly, we began to trust each other as well.

CHAPTER 8

I'm Not a Little Kid!

Each man must love his wife as he loves himself,
and the wife must respect her husband.

Ephesians 5:33

Him

I really don't like being told what to do. You can call it a rebellious streak, stubbornness, or rugged independence, but I have this compulsive desire to do things my way. It's not that I can't see other points of view or follow someone else's lead. It's just that with my independent spirit I don't always think to ask. And when I feel strongly about a point of view or a course of action, I can be downright immovable.

I take my responsibilities seriously. But if I'm faced with something I think won't be successful or that I won't enjoy doing, I drag my feet. This drives Jen *crazy*.

This book is a great example. If I had a dollar for every time Jen asked me to write or asked me if I planned on writing, we'd be financially secure.

Given the strong-willed nature of my personality, it must have been great fun for my parents to raise me. Now that I have children of my own, I can get some sense of the frustration my parents must have felt with trying to bend my will to theirs. Bill Cosby once talked about "The Mother's Curse," which goes something like this: "I hope when you grow up and have kids that they act exactly how you act."

When we get together with my parents, after the hugs, kisses, and pleasantries, the conversation soon turns to telling stories about the family. "Remember that time?" or "That reminds of when you . . ." or "I wonder whatever happened to so-and-so? Y'all were always getting into something." We enjoy telling those old stories. Even though the favorites are repeated over and over, no one really seems to mind or gets tired of telling or hearing them. Those tales are destined to become the stuff of legend with our grandchildren.

A favorite story of my parents' and kids' centers on the struggles that Mom and Dad had trying to get me to go to bed. As an infant, I would play, talk, or sing to myself—anything I could do to keep from falling asleep. When all else had failed, I would pull myself up in my crib and cry until I threw up.

So how does all this fit into the context of marriage and relationships? Well, Jen has learned that telling me to do something is a guaranteed way *not* to get me to do it. She realized that she couldn't dictate what I should do, but that I needed to collaborate and fully buy into the parameters we put in place to help me with my porn addiction. This did not come easy for her. She may tell you that she is still learning it, especially when her fears kick into overdrive.

What God Has Put Together

When I met Jen, I could tell she was the typical "type A" personality. Imagine Monica on the TV show *Friends* (and no, I'm not Chandler). Everything has its place and nothing makes her happier than a clean and organized house. On the other hand, I'm a master of controlled chaos. The only organized parts of my life involve my work, but that is only out of necessity, and it's not all the time.

I'm a firm believer that God put us together, but I also believe that God has an incredible sense of humor. While Jen's life was very regimented when we first met, mine was fairly loose. For example, Jen kept thorough financial records and had never been late or missed a payment for anything. I think I have balanced my checkbook once, maybe twice. You can guess who pays the bills in our household.

Even though we seem so different in a lot of ways, Jen and I have each made a concerted effort to keep Jesus at the center of our marriage. Christ is the glue that holds us together. This point is absolutely paramount. If you want your marriage to work, God has to be the foundation and at the center. Jesus—God's Son— said this: "I am the way, the truth, and the life. No one can come to the Father except through me" (John 14:6). Both Jen and I have found that we reach out to Jesus when we can't or won't reach out to each other. I have seen God do some amazing things in our marriage as a result. I truly believe He will do the same for you.

As our marriage has grown, so have Jen and I. We've moved closer to one another. Jen has become more laid back and I have learned to be a bit more responsible. I'm not just saying that because she asked me to either.

This is another vital point, especially in marriage. Are you growing toward your spouse or are you growing apart? How can you tell? Do yourselves and your marriage a favor. Take a moment to talk to each other about your respective spiritual growth. What are you struggling with and where do you feel God is moving in your life?

With Jen and me, the movement and growth were really subtle, so much so that we often had to look for it to spot it. We decided to start encouraging one another when we saw God moving in each other.

You have to be intentional when working on your relationship. Make it a point to look for the good in one another. Don't be quick to point out faults. Jesus talked about not saying anything to your brother (or sister) about the speck of dust in his or her eye without first removing the plank in your own.[1] On any given day, I could have a redwood forest growing there, so I try to keep the blame-tossing to a minimum.

When in Doubt, Talk It Out

Occasionally, I'll do something that Jen doesn't like or I won't do something that she has asked me to do. At the beginning of our marriage, this would have resulted in a lecture from Jen on how I might "hear" her but I don't really "listen" to her. That's if she was in a good mood. If she wasn't, the lecture would turn into something more serious. Either way, fights were rare then and usually are now. Jen is an outward processor. I'm an inward processor. This means that she wants to talk it out and I want to mull it over and think on it a bit—so we often talk it out. I have noticed recently, though, that Jen is giving me more time and space to turn around the discussion in my mind. When this happens, the conversations go *much* better. More growth!

When in the midst of the occasional lecture session, I often feel talked down to by Jen. She is trained as a teacher, and every now and then the teacher voice will come out. I don't respond well to that. It doesn't make me feel respected. Instead, I feel parented. When this happens, I don't feel as if she sees me as an equal. I put up the defensive walls and try to wait her out. Since Jen likes to have things settled, waiting her out isn't always an option.

Once Jen made the angry comment that she felt as if she had three kids instead of two. That one stung a bit. I usually just take such jabs, but underneath I seethe. This is not healthy. The pressure builds and builds until I blow my top. It doesn't happen very often, but when it does, *wow*!

What I finally realized is that as a child, I often rebelled against my parents and their authority. Now, I found myself rebelling against the very things Jen *and I* put in place to help me with my addiction. I wasn't rebelling against Jen. I was rebelling against the notion I needed rules to live by, at least when it came to porn. Full confession: I agreed to these parameters in the first place just to get her to stop talking about my addiction. Although part of me wanted to be healed, a large part of me was not yet willing to be.

Some specific instances stick out when I felt Jen was acting more as a parent than a partner. The first instance was after her initial discovery of my porn use. I could tell that Jen was walking on eggshells around me. I sensed her eyes constantly watching me, even when they weren't. I had to keep doors open. It seemed like every time I got up off the couch she was asking me where I was going and what I was doing. It was stifling and annoying.

Now that I look back and reflect on it, I have some understanding of where she was coming from. Jen was scared. She felt her role was to protect our marriage and to protect me from myself.

But there is a fundamental flaw with this logic. The role of protector belongs, ultimately, to *God*. All that is required of you is your obedience to His Word and promptings. There is nothing you can do to control the other person's actions. No amount of talking, begging, pleading, nagging, yelling, or crying will help you be successful in this endeavor. You have to release that to God.

Jen finally came to that conclusion. Not only did it do wonders for our relationship, it granted her more freedom than she could have imagined. She let God take over the disciplining. She let God speak words of encouragement and love over me. Jen allowed God to be my parent, while she embraced her role as partner and wife. Jen prayed for and with me. She asked others to do the same. She challenged me to assume the role of spiritual head of the family. In other words, she asked me to step it up.

When this happened, there was a fundamental shift in our communication and our relationship. I didn't feel parented anymore. I felt loved and respected. I felt as if Jen was beginning to trust me again. This was huge! Since trust is crucial to a relationship, I responded. I found myself wanting to do more and talk to Jen more about what was going on with me. I started sharing with her about when I felt tempted. Our conversations evolved from worrying about what to do about temptation to discussing strategies to help me overcome it when it actually came. I began to trust and love her more than I had before.

Love Is Spelled R-E-S-P-E-C-T

Men need respect. It's built into all of us. Men also need their spouses. After all, God said at the beginning that it isn't good for us to be alone.[2] We have to be able to communicate with our spouses, and our dialogue should be built on respect and love, especially when there is conflict in the relationship. Dr. Emerson Eggerichs goes so far as to say, "Men need to feel respected during conflict more than they need to feel loved."[3] Many wives desire to feel deeply and greatly loved. Both love and respect can be given through the words we choose to say to one another, as well as the words we do not say. Nothing can be taboo or forbidden. Once you start keeping secrets from one another, you are giving the enemy a foothold.

Jen has often asked me if I mind talking about my pornography addiction. I've told her no and here's why: It's the shame, the darkness, and the desire to keep it hidden that gives pornography its power. The only way to defeat it is to expose it and to bring it into the light. As Ephesians 5:10–11 says, "Carefully determine what pleases the Lord. Take no part in the worthless deeds of evil and darkness; instead, expose them." God wants us to talk about it. It was one of the reasons we started writing this book.

Just as God wants me to talk about my porn addiction to expose it to the light, He also wants to bring His light to anything else that hinders our marriage. If you feel disrespected by your wife, talk to her about it. She might get defensive. She might make excuses. She might tell you a thousand things you are doing wrong. But you can't control how she is going to react. All you can do is bring up the issue in love and trust that God will use your words to plant a seed in her heart.

If we choose not to have conversations because we are afraid of how the other person will react, we will choose to allow bitterness to take root in our own heart. And this bitterness breeds more quickly than rabbits. The more you communicate the better off you will be. You might find that different ways of communicating work better than others. Finding your communication style may be by trial and error. That's okay. No one is demanding perfection. You may not see results at first, but that's okay too. Trust God with the growth process.

You may ask, "Why should I put myself at risk for a possible blow-up?" Because you're fighting for your marriage. Your wife is your partner. It's hard to fight the enemy while fighting with each other. You need to build a firm bond that the enemy can't break.

You do that by taking time daily for each other and learning how to communicate effectively.

One of the books I found that was really helpful for Jen and me was *The Five Love Languages* by Gary Chapman. The premise behind the book is that we all feel loved in different ways. If you want to make your spouse feel loved, then you have to speak his or her respective love language. Jen and I both read it early on in our marriage. Through the years, it has done wonders for building strong communication, but it takes practice to put the principles into effect. Many times, you don't think to love in a way differently than you receive love. It takes intentional practice to love in a way that isn't necessarily instinctual. For example, my love language is "words of affirmation." Jen's love language is "quality time." I don't need as much deeply connective conversation as Jen does, but I have learned to value it because she does. Jen doesn't automatically offer praise to me for a job well done, but she has come to recognize over time how powerfully that builds me up. She also realizes how quickly I can let criticism take me down. She's learning to weigh what is really important and approach me gently. We both mess up in how we love each other sometimes, but it's worth putting in the effort to perfect.

Remember what's important. Talk to each other. Love each other and respect each other's views. Forgive each other. Your recovery is a process and it takes time and patience. Most importantly, pray with and for each other. Nothing is more powerful.

CHAPTER 9

When God's in Charge

I pray that God, the source of hope, will fill you completely with joy and peace because you trust in him. Then you will overflow with confident hope through the power of the Holy Spirit.

Romans 15:13

For so long in this process of porn addiction, both Craig and I have felt tremendous amounts of hopelessness. For those of you who are visual learners, picture a room of blackness or an insurmountable brick wall. There is this desire to wade through the darkness, find the door, and let in light. There is a notion that if we could just get to the top of the wall and look over, we would find a land of freedom and peace. But at some point in the battle, we tire of always running our hands along the wall, searching for the knob. Our hands and feet go limp while trying to find the next foothold that will help give us a boost in the climb.

We start to feel defeated. We think we will never win. We begin to lose hope. We've spent all this time searching for recovery and just when we think we've found it, something happens. We lose the light, the wall gets taller, and the land of freedom and peace never materializes like we thought it would.

Hopeless

Both Craig and I came to the understanding somewhere in the process that our hope had been tied up in the wrong place. We became hopeless because our efforts to recover from porn addiction had failed. Recovery had become our hope. Recovery had been our sign that we could find joy, happiness, and intimacy in our marriage again. And so, when the process of recovery failed, so did our chances, our hope, of having a sustainable, loving marriage.

But the truth is, our ability to communicate and walk together in this marriage cannot be based solely on our behaviors and choices. Our recovery and resisting temptation—these are in flux. As much as we depend on God to make recovery real and true in our lives, we also know that there is a human element in the mix. We are not perfect. We will mess up. We will make the wrong choice at some point. We will fall into sin. And even if we don't succumb to temptation to look at porn or engage in controlling behavior, there is the possibility that someday we could.

How can we continue to not just survive but thrive, even in the midst of struggle in our marriage?

The answer? We can't lose hope. And in order to not lose hope, we have to figure out what it is and where it comes from.

What Is Hope?

The secular definition of hope is this: "the feeling that what is wanted can be had or that events will turn out for the best."[1] *Hope* has become a synonym for *wish*. If we look at hope through the lens of Scripture, we find there is an added clause. Yes, hope is "a confident expectation for the future, describing both the act of hoping and the object hoped for."[2] But more than that, hope—when rooted in God—allows us to press on to live in the way that He desires us to live, even when we have trouble and experience hardship.

Hope is not a destination. We don't make it to the end of a process and think, "Now, we can have hope." Rather, hope is what *gets us* to our destination. It is the fuel that keeps us going even when the future looks bleak. It is what compels us to keep trying, even when the task looks insurmountable. It is that which keeps us afloat when we are drowning in a stormy sea.

Where does this hope lie? Only in God. He is the source.

Wearing Hope

The battle of porn addiction can leave one feeling shipwrecked. The life you have built together seems to have a crack in the hull. The waves of trouble from the porn crash horrifically on an already battered ship. Pretty soon, the marriage begins to founder. You're taking on too much water and you find that you are sinking. You're drowning in despair, guilt, and fear.

Have you ever seen someone drowning? They bob up and down, desperate for air. Their arms move, trying to grasp and hold on to the surface of the water. They can't call for help because they are having trouble breathing. They seem stuck in the same spot, not able to move closer to shore. They are caught in a vise of panic.

Just like a drowning human being, a marriage that has been swamped by porn addiction needs rescue. While the process of rescue from the clutches of porn is often a long process, God knows that we need something to keep us afloat while He rebuilds our ship, our marriage. So He gives us hope. He is what keeps our heads above water while the storm rages. He is, in essence, our lifejacket, or our boat's lifesaving anchor in the storm.

Let's look at Hebrews 6:13–19:

> For example, there was God's promise to Abraham. Since there was no one greater to swear by, God took an oath in his own name, saying:
>
> "I will certainly bless you, and I will multiply your descendants beyond number."
>
> Then Abraham waited patiently, and he received what God had promised.
>
> Now when people take an oath, they call on someone greater than themselves to hold them to it. And without any question that oath is binding. God also bound himself with an oath, so that those who received the promise could be perfectly sure that he would never change his mind. So God has given both his promise and his oath. These two things are unchangeable because it is impossible for God to lie. Therefore, we who have fled to him for refuge can have great confidence as we hold to the hope that lies before us. *This hope is a strong and trustworthy anchor for our souls.* It leads us through the curtain into God's inner sanctuary. (emphasis mine)

Our process of recovery is subject to human nature (i.e., sin). But God's promise of hope is not. God's character does not change based on our performance. This means that He will not change His mind about offering us hope. In fact, not only does He not change His mind, He has set it up so that He cannot. His perfect nature will not allow it. In Jeremiah 29:11–13, God says He knows the plans He has for His people, and He says "they are plans for good and not for disaster, to give you a future and a *hope*." In this passage, God is speaking to the Israelites who have been exiled from their land and held captive by a foreign king. God is promising them that despite their bleak situation and their lack of vision for how to get out of their current circumstances, He is going to bring them back home. Pornography is this foreign king holding your marriage captive, but God has plans to bring you back together to wholeness, for your home to be a place of safety. He gives you hope to hold on to until this deliverance becomes your reality.

Let's return to Hebrews 6:18. God says that we can flee to Him for refuge, and when we do this, we can have great confidence as we hold on to His hope. I took refuge at first in my own control of Craig and in the rules that we had put in place to keep him "safe" from porn. Clearly, that was not a safe harbor for me or for him. While rules can be broken and security measures derailed, our refuge in God can never be anything other than foolproof.

What does the refuge of God look like? In my research of this verse, I came across this commentary that specifically speaks to the historical meaning behind *"fled to him for refuge."* It refers the six cities of refuge in the Old Testament. Each of these cities' names has a particular meaning. These meanings describe the type of refuge that God is and allow us to see how what we have been running to for protection pales in comparison to the shelter of God. The chart below shows you the cities and the meanings of their names, with a brief description of how this relates to God as our refuge.[3]

City	Name meaning	Description of meaning
Kadesh	holy	Implies the holiness of God, that He is set apart from the world.
Shechem	shoulder	Taken from Isaiah 9:6, describing Jesus as Wonderful Counselor, Mighty God, Everlasting Father, Prince of Peace.
Hebron	fellowship	We are called into fellowship with Christ.
Bezer	fortress	Christ is a fortress to all who trust in Him.
Ramoth	high	God has exalted Jesus with His right hand.
Golan	joy	In Christ, we are justified and shall live in glory with Him.

I think about all the time I wasted living in my Jen-made shelters I thought would protect my marriage from porn. And I think about all the times Craig sought refuge *in* porn in order to escape his own sense of drowning in rejection, shame, and inadequacies. No wonder we felt so hopeless. But God is gracious and He knows what we need—a safe place to seek Him while He works in us to change our course from running to those false shelters that we have built in our lives. He shows us that He is holy, perfect, a wonderful counselor. We can never go wrong when we flee to Him when the storm torments us.

As we flee to Him for refuge, He equips us to weather the storm with hope—His hope! Back to Hebrews: In verse 18, the author writes we "can have great confidence as we hold to the hope that lies before us." The Greek word used in the original Bible text for "can have" is *echo*, which means, "to wear." Essentially, we are wearing His hope, clinging to it as a life preserver, to keep us from drowning while enduring the storm that is porn addiction. And we can cling to this with great confidence because it comes from God. It will never run out. It will never go away. It will never fail. All we need to do is hold on. When we choose not to let go of God and the hope that He gives us, we can survive the shipwreck, even when it looks like our immediate circumstances are not changing. Even when we still feel lost at sea.

As we hold on, clinging to the hope He promises us, it allows us to continue moving forward in our lives, both individually and as a couple. In the NIV translation of verse 18, it says, "We who have fled to take hold of the hope *set before us* may be greatly encouraged." The Greek word for "set before us" is the same word used in Hebrews 12:1–2 (*prokeimai*) where it talks about running the race that God has *marked out for us* (NIV). When we grab the hope that is set before us, we can carry on together with perseverance, with patient endurance, fixing our eyes on Christ, who will perfect our faith. Jesus endured the cross because of the joy that would come after His death and resurrection. We can persevere through this storm, too, because with Jesus there is always hope. We can live with joy in our relationship in Him, despite the circumstances that enter our lives. Not only did He die to take away our sins, He promises to be with us on each step of that journey. We can always move forward in our journey with Jesus as our hope.

Finally, Paul describes this hope, comparing it to a strong and trustworthy anchor. When we are tethered to God, we are assured that we will not drift aimlessly off to sea, even as the storm swirls around us. We are deeply rooted in Him. He is the one who can keep us grounded in love for our spouse. He is the one who can help us see our spouse as a child of God and not just a control or porn freak. He is the one who can change our perspective from one of despair to one of joy, even in the midst of a horrendous struggle. With God all things are possible, even if this runs contrary to your logic. So often we get bogged down by what we see physically happening on this earth. But there is so much more. Sarah Young, in her devotional *Jesus Calling*, takes the Scripture found in 2 Corinthians 4:17–18, and words it like this:

> It is impossible for you to have a need that I cannot meet. After all, I created you and everything that is. The world is still at my beck and call, though it often appears otherwise. Do not be fooled by appearances. *Things that are visible are brief and fleeting, while things that are invisible are everlasting.*

Despite what we see, we can have hope in a God who is always working in our hearts to draw us closer to Him. So many times I looked at Craig, didn't see God working, and promptly lost hope. If only I had clung to the confident hope that God does not abandon us, that He never stops talking to us and loving us, that He never stops pursuing us. If I had seen him with that perspective, I could have given up my anger and control so much more easily.

And so many times Craig looked at me and saw me as a controlling wife who only wanted him to be whipped into shape. If he had only clung to the confident hope that God was in the process of soothing my fearful heart, opening my hands and helping me to release all things to Him. If he had seen me with that perspective, he could have let down the rebellious façade and trusted that deep down my heart was really for him.

For you to discuss together:

1. Think about the feeling of being shipwrecked, tossed about by the waves, with the threat of drowning. What is the first thing you reach for to save you? What do you reach for in the metaphorical storms of life?

2. Have those things been effective in the past? Are they healthy things that God uses to sustain you or are they antithetical to His nature and purpose?

3. When you think of refuge, what or whom do you run to for safety? Again, are those places or people that God uses to help you? Or are you seeking shelter in things of this world?

4. Do you believe God's hope can sustain you even when the situation looks bleak? How can you foster the practice of holding on to biblical truth when feelings of despair threaten you?

PART 4

Rebuilding Trust

CHAPTER 10

The First Real Confession

Forgiveness is the fragrance that the violet sheds on the heel that has crushed it.

Mark Twain

■ Her

It was a regular day. The kids were already in school. Craig was getting ready for work. I was plugging along, working on my computer. I stopped to ask him a question about something, calling to him from the dining room into the kitchen. I can't remember what I asked, but I do remember it led to this follow-up question: "When was the last time you looked at porn?" There was no anger or accusation in my voice. I was used to asking this question. What I was not used to was the answer that followed.

For the first time in the history of our marriage, Craig actually answered me honestly: "Last month, when I was traveling," he said. "I'm sorry I've hurt you again."

(Oh, those hotel rooms! Such traps. Satan leads him to believe that if he does it there, in the solitude and confines of the cookie-cutter hotel room, his secret will never see the light of day.)

In this moment, I had two choices: I could give in to the anger and fear, which threatened to overtake me . . . or I could rejoice in this moment of truth.

My quick inner monologue started: *I know you're mad, but if you react harshly, he might not tell you the truth again.*

I weighed out a response. To take joy in the confession would be harder in the moment but more fruitful for our marriage. To react with anger would be easier in the moment but would make our marriage and journey through this much more difficult.

I chose to delay my yearning for instantaneous gratification and reject the desire of my worldly self, which so badly wanted to explode, and if I'm completely honest, berate him for his bad decision. I decided not to give in to my temptation to throw his words back in his face with a question like *"How many other times have you lied to me when I've asked you if you fell into temptation?"*

The decision was rooted in what I valued more—perceived victory or brutal honesty. In reality, most of the times that Craig has said he defeated temptation and didn't look at porn, I didn't *fully* believe him anyway (which is why I say "perceived victory"). Superficially, I could accept his response, but it usually left me with inner turmoil and doubt. Not until he started pursuing Jesus could I put any weight on his statements and begin to stand on them as the truth. And even now when we talk about it, my stomach churns and I wonder. It takes a long time to heal from lies.

As with any addiction there are steps toward recovery, and this one sounds much like step five of the Twelve Steps of Alcoholics Anonymous: "(We) admitted to God, to ourselves, and to another human being the exact nature of our wrongs."[1] Even though it felt like we were taking a million steps back (*porn use so recently?*), perhaps we were actually taking a few steps forward. Our feelings do not always give us the fullness of the situation. We need God to reveal the whole truth to us.

And here is the truth of the situation: For the first time, Craig was coming *to* me to repent and ask my forgiveness. I wasn't pulling an apology *from* him. He wasn't forced to apologize on the spot as when I caught him all the times before. He could have just lied again and avoided this whole conversation.

God helped me see that what Craig offered me was a gift I had never received before: unadulterated truth. No, it had not come wrapped in the prettiest of papers, but the gift itself was priceless. Like any gift-giver, he or she wants it to be received with grace and gratitude. Any shunning or disdain might prompt him or her never to give again, or at least, not any time soon. And so, with grace and gratitude, I took his truth and I rejoiced. As painful as it was, I rejoiced.

Truth—no matter what the truth—is better than a lie, especially within the context of a marriage. Truth allows light to enter dark places. And where there is light, there is progress. So no matter how troublesome and dismal the truth, the very utterance of it breathes hope.

And yet . . . the truth still hurts. Even though he brought confession and repentance, there is still the aftermath of my own feelings of betrayal. And I must remember that while God gave me the grace to accept those gifts from Craig, God also knows my heart needs time to grieve and to heal. There is a process of my own recovery that I need to talk out with God.

I imagine all those times when Craig lied to me and I equate it to being in a closet with the light off and the door shut. When he opened the door and let in the light—when he exposed his truth—my eyes squinted and the light felt painful for a moment as I became accustomed to the brightness.

Just as my eyes have to adjust to light, my heart needs time to adjust to truth. And God is the One who helps me make this adjustment. Without Him helping me through this process, I would stew in my internal anger.

The Burden of Anger

For many years of our marriage, I chose to sit in anger. On the outside, it didn't look like I harbored anything. As you may have already guessed, I didn't mince my words after catching Craig when our firstborn was just a few months old. I easily became consumed with my anger, and there was no hesitancy to let it fuel the fiery words that spewed out of my mouth.

But if you remember, the first episode quickly turned south as Craig started making suicidal comments. In order to help him out of this dark place, I had to push my anger out of the way to allow compassion and love to enter in. My focus became saving Craig and I didn't have time to deal with my own emotions any longer. It was by God's grace that I was able to love him through this process and speak truth to him, even though my own inner turmoil roiled.

When the storm died down, I believed if I could say these things to him and say I had forgiven him, I shouldn't be angry anymore. So I tried my best to ignore those emotions, containing them in a shoebox placed on a high shelf. By the time that tumultuous Mother's Day arrived, I did all my railing at God instead of at Craig. But I was still railing, the anger crashing over me like an overpowering wave. Just like waves, if anger doesn't have the proper outlet, it can feel untamable as it seeps into all aspects of our lives.

What I realized with my anger is that there is a reason for the expression "blow your top." That lid that tries to cover your anger? It's not very strong against anger's power to expand and overwhelm over time, especially if that anger has been neglected and ignored. I was afraid to share with Craig on a heart-level how angry his porn addiction made me—perhaps because I was afraid it would trigger the suicidal thoughts or remind him that porn is an issue.

Even though I got mad at God for allowing me to marry a porn addict, it never crossed my mind that I needed His help dealing with my anger. But then, with all the anger bottled up, I would explode over inconsequential things. Or, if I had legitimate cause to be angry at something he did, my reaction would often be stronger than it should have been. Neglected anger usually comes out.

For example, if Craig left a dish on the counter, I would say his behavior devalued me. (Couldn't he realize how much I already did around the house? Couldn't he take five extra seconds to put it in the dishwasher?) When he didn't call because he was running late, I would tell him he was being irresponsible and he must not care that I worried incessantly. When he wasn't playing with the kids because he was playing video games, I told him he wasn't being a good dad or a good husband because if he was, clearly he would choose us over some "shoot-'em-up" game every single time. I would never see another reason for his choices. I would never try to see things from his point of view. There was no grace to give because I let my unresolved anger issues make everything about me. Because I felt unsatisfied about being able to talk about what was really hurting me and because I did not involve God in this aspect of my life, I used some very trivial incidents to justify permitting some of my anger to leak out of my consumed soul.

Let me tell you—this is an unproductive way to manage your anger and your relationship and yourself. Here is the irony: I was angry with Craig for hiding his porn use, and yet here I was hiding my anger. My secret anger was becoming just as destructive as his secret porn use.

And so, just as I learned I had to give up Craig's porn addiction to God, I had to learn to give Him my anger, too. Only God could help me figure out what to do with it because clearly, I was

PURE EYES, CLEAN HEART

not doing a good job on my own. Through the process of giving up anger, I could give in to the idea of forgiveness.

Trading Anger for Forgiveness

Anger is a burden. I imagine carrying a weighted sack on my back. I take a moment to feel the heaviness of it. I try to walk with it. What changes? My gait. My posture. My speed. Choosing to carry my anger around slows me down from actually healing from the pain. Eventually, I get too tired to keep walking toward reconciliation with my husband or into the arms of Jesus. I get nowhere and my only company is my rage.

And so, ultimately, I am left with a choice. I can make anger my friend or I can abandon it for something else: my God and, eventually, my husband.

I put down the rock that is my anger and I leave it by the side of the road. And, over time, I lay out all my fears to God, fears which have for so long justified my limping around, walking in circles. My conversations with Him go something like this:

Me: If I give up my anger and forgive him, he'll think that I think his addiction is not really a big deal.

God: "Short-tempered people do foolish things, and schemers are hated" (Proverbs 14:17).

Me: So what you're telling me is it's not my concern how he takes the forgiveness, and the anger is actually doing more harm than good to our relationship? Because the truth is, I have schemed to try to catch him and manipulated events so I could seem to be in

the right. And many times, I have said and done foolish things out of anger.

God: "Get rid of all bitterness, rage, anger, harsh words,
        and slander, as well as all types of evil behavior.
        Instead, be kind to each other, tenderhearted, forgiv-
        ing one another, just as God through Christ has for-
        given you" (Ephesians 4:31–32).

Me: So if I choose not to forgive Craig, I am walking in
        disobedience to you?

God: "If you forgive those who sin against you, your heav-
        enly Father will forgive you. But if you refuse to for-
        give others, your Father will not forgive your sins"
        (Matthew 6:14–15).

This last line is crushing to me, because I know how much I
need forgiveness daily. The very thought of not being able to have
access to that forgiveness and grace is unnerving. And I know how
many poor choices I have made in speaking and relating to my
husband. I know I have sinned against him when I've sought to be
controlling. I know I've said awful things that made him feel like a
child all because I thought somehow this was the way to get him to
turn from porn. I know I need his forgiveness, too, and what would
it be like for me if he chose to harbor anger instead of forgiving me?

I need continual forgiveness. I wasn't controlling just *once*. I
didn't manipulate only *once*. I didn't say mean things *once*. Even
after I had confessed and apologized, I still found myself returning
to old behaviors because I got scared and chose not to trust God.

Sounds like my husband and I are quite the same in this area.

It sounds like we are both greatly in need of grace, and having a wall of anger between us only separates us from the person and the God we love most.

It is the awareness of how far short I fall on a daily basis that reminds me of how to have grace so that when confessions come, when repentance is offered, I can receive them with open arms and allow God to help me deal with my own hurt in the aftermath. This is true in situations other than porn use. Any time Craig hurts me, I can choose not to respond in anger. I can ask God to teach me how to react differently, how to be tenderhearted and kind, even when I am in pain. He can teach me how to speak to him so my feelings are heard, but in a constructive way that doesn't heap more aching on either heart. And He can teach Craig the same thing. But both of us have to be willing not to choose what feels the best in the moment. If we don't choose well, the flesh will almost always win.

Forgiveness Is for *You*

No matter what your husband believes about his porn use, you can still practice forgiveness in your relationship with him. Some of you may have a husband who came to you with his battle and repented of it before you even knew there was a problem. Some of you are like me who have a husband who hid his porn use and you stumbled upon it. Some of you have a husband who, whether he is open about it or not, refuses to apologize for it because he has yet to see anything wrong with it. Whether he asks for your forgiveness or he doesn't, you can still forgive.

Offering your husband forgiveness doesn't mean you excuse his behavior. It doesn't make his porn use right. It doesn't make you a doormat. It doesn't give him permission to continue to engage in this wanton fantasy world.

Offering forgiveness also does not offer you any protection he won't engage in pornography usage again. It's not an insurance policy by any stretch of the imagination, even if he has come to you and repented. While the dictionary definition of *repent* is "to feel such sorrow for sin or fault as to be disposed to change one's life for the better,"[2] the pull of the addiction can sometimes overshadow the desire to change course.

Even though receiving your forgiveness can be helpful to him and for your marriage, the giving of forgiveness is exceedingly beneficial for you and your own relationship with God. Without Jesus' sacrifice for us, none of us would have the relationship we have with God today. We are all sinners, desperate for His grace. And if we want it, we must be willing to give it.

CHAPTER 11

Why Your Wife Is Not Your Enemy

*People who conceal their sins will not prosper,
but if they confess and turn from them, they will
receive mercy.*

Proverbs 28:13

▨ Him

Pride is such a terrible thing, yet it seems inherent to our sense of masculinity. It's so hard for us men to admit we're wrong. We "need" to be right. We want to be justified in our feelings and actions.

But how can we *really* be right and justified? We want to live a life as sin-free as possible, but every single day we fail in some way. I find myself feeling that this "sin-free" ideal sets the bar so high I can never reach it.

Thank God for Jesus! Thank God for His grace! Jesus makes it okay that I can't reach perfection. He makes it okay that I am not right all of the time. And once I realize that it's okay for me to be imperfect, how can I have any different expectations for my wife?

I have to remember my spouse is as broken as I am. Just as I don't want to admit I am wrong, Jen doesn't want to say, "I forgive you." It hurts too much. She feels like she is saying my porn addiction is okay, even though that is not the truth.

Forgiveness sometimes feels like surrendering, and that can be scary. The world tells us that surrendering is a bad thing. However, surrender is a necessary part of reconciliation. We have to push through our own guilt and pain, and instead draw toward one another in order to forgive. It's hard! But it's well worth the effort.

I came across a story about a man who had lived a very sinful lifestyle for a long time. Eventually he gave his heart to Christ and married a Christian woman. One day he told her about his past, and wondered how she could forgive him. She told him, "John, I want you to know that here in my arms is your home. When I married you I married your old nature as well as your new nature."[1]

Can you picture yourself as the man in this story? Can you picture yourself as his wife? What an amazing display of trust in each other and in God. I realize this story illustrates the ideal, but the point is this: We should be willing to ask for forgiveness and equally willing to forgive. That is a necessary step in recovery for both husband and wife.

When we fall back into pornography, we may feel like we've returned to step one. I've been there so many times. Like a child who is first learning to walk, we make mistakes. We're going to fall.

When we fall, God is *always* going to be there to pick us up *but only if we let Him*. We have to reach out to Him. He will forgive us, but we must initiate the confession. The old proverb is true: "If you don't feel God near to you, He is not the one who moved." Your recovery is dependent on your daily walk with God and Jesus.

You cannot win this battle alone. If you have been blessed with a spouse, it is God who has given you your partner. You have to work together as a team in order to be successful, not just in overcoming porn addiction, but in doing life. Victory starts with being vulnerable with each other. And that requires honesty—with yourself and with your spouse. There is power in the truth. Truth creates the opportunity to be forgiven.

He Already Knows, So Why Do I Hide?

The first step is recognizing our true nature. As long as we are on this earth, we will be sinful and therefore, at war with our own flesh. Since you are reading this book, you or someone close to you is likely struggling with porn. But everyone has struggles. It can be alcohol, drugs, sex, pride, or anything that we have set up as an idol instead of seeking after God and his will. Victory starts with us being willing to lay down everything that we call "ours" and giving it to God.

I often chase after my own hopes and dreams. I strive for that next promotion. I continually look for that next car or house. I keep telling myself, "As soon as I have (insert item here) I'll be satisfied." The problem is that there is nothing I can obtain, neither status nor object, that can replace God. I end up hiding from the very thing that has the power to give me the true desires of my heart.

There is a Latin phrase that translates, "Not to us, Lord, but to your name give glory."[2] What does this really mean? It's a reminder that my own pride is an enemy. The image I have of myself is fleeting. My reputation is a papier-mâché mask that can be crushed or destroyed in an instant. As the author of Ecclesiastes wrote, "I observed everything going on under the sun, and really, it is all meaningless—like chasing the wind" (Ecclesiastes 1:14).

At one time or another, we all experience the exasperation conveyed in that Scripture. Why do we chase the wind? Why do we feel the need to satisfy our own desires instead of God's? Why is it so hard to do what is right when we know that the wages of sin is death? Why do we try to hide from the One who sees everything?

I've asked myself these questions repeatedly. There is good news though. In Psalm 139:1–4, the psalmist David wrote, "O LORD, you have examined my heart and know everything about me. You know when I sit down or stand up. You know my thoughts even when I'm far away. . . . You know what I'm going to say even before I say it."

God knows our hearts. He knows our thoughts before we even think them. He even knew our entire lives before creation. He knew about every sin, every trial, every victory, and every defeat. Yet in spite of all of our failures, He stills stands by us and wants a deeper relationship with us.

As a kid, I occasionally got into trouble. (Who didn't?) I recall the lectures, scoldings, and punishments my parents used to discipline me. I would often feel pretty guilty about what I had done. When my parents asked me why I did what I did or what I was thinking when I did it, my response was generally the same: "I don't know." But there is something they always said that encouraged me: "Craig, there is nothing you can do that would keep us from loving you."

I finally realized that God is saying the same thing to me, over and over: "There is nothing you can do to keep me from loving you. Stop hiding from Me." That is an amazing feeling!

One day I was really down on myself, wracked with guilt and self-pity. I cried out to God asking Him, "Why? Why is this such a struggle? Why can't I be successful? Why am I such a failure?" I sensed His response, "You're my son. The son of the Most High King. Start acting like it."

I was taken aback. I was not used to God speaking to me that firmly. And I could tell that He was in no mood to hear any more of my moaning and groaning. He wanted my attention and He got it!

As I think back on that, it was exactly what I needed to hear. God is like that. He knows what we need before we even know it. I'm in awe of the extent of His grace and mercy. But remember, God created us in His image. It's time we start acting like it. Ask for His forgiveness, believe it, and then act like His forgiven son.

Don't Hide from Her Either

Back to confessing to your wife. There is something holy about the act of confession. Jen and I are members of the Episcopal Church. It's the American branch of the Anglican Communion. In the church, we have seven sacraments. One of them is called "confession and absolution." As part of our liturgy we also use *The Book of Common Prayer*. Inside the book is a rite of reconciliation, which you can do with a member of the clergy or even another layperson.

Obviously, confession doesn't have to be a formal rite. James 5:16 simply tells us, "Confess your sins to each other and pray for each other so that you may be healed. The earnest prayer of a righteous person has great power and produces wonderful results." Confession can simply be a conversation between you and a trusted friend. Don't get so caught up in what to say or how to say it. Just open your mouth and let the Holy Spirit guide you. What is important is that you do it.

God wants us to confess our sins. He wants to lift the burdens off our shoulders. The act of confession shines God's light into the darkness of our hearts. It opens the doors to His grace and mercy. If you don't ask for it, how can you possibly receive it?

It's hard for men to share what's going on inside their heads and hearts, but who better to share your most intimate thoughts with than your wife? After all, you and your spouse are one flesh. God has joined you together. Sin causes separation between you and God; it also separates you from your wife. The act of confession restores that relationship. It creates anew the wholeness. As the line from the marriage ceremony proclaims, "What God has put together, let no one put asunder." That includes us. We should look for ways to maintain our wholeness with our spouse. This means being honest about the hard stuff. The stuff you really want to hide. The stuff that you are convincing yourself is better left in the dark.

I know it's hard to be vulnerable. Being a man means we're not supposed to ask for directions. We're not supposed to cry. We don't make mistakes (at least nothing we'll admit to). To do any of these things means we are less than the man we are supposed to be. But these commonly accepted ideas about men have their roots in pride and they are a false view of what true masculinity really is. Real masculinity puts others in front of self and is not afraid to be intimate or genuine. True manhood is rooted in integrity and seeks the truth no matter how hard it may be to hear.

God has called us to be in relationship with Him and with our spouse. We cannot accomplish that and live day after day in the sin of pornography. The two are completely and utterly incompatible. There are countless stories of divorce and separation caused by pornography addictions. According to an article in *Psychology Today*, porn is the cause of roughly 500,000 divorces annually.[3] That alone should be enough to get our attention.

There is no need to become a statistic. The answer is right in front of you. When you first fell in love with your spouse, you may have felt frightened. I know I was. I was terrified that Jen did not feel the same way about me that I felt about her. I remember calling one of my best friends and talking it out with him for over two hours. Talking things out really helped me. Back then, fear didn't keep me from asking Jen to marry me. It shouldn't keep me from doing everything in my power to *stay* married to her, including confessing my sins to her. The act actually brings the two of you closer together.

It took a lot for me to actually confess to Jen when I had fallen down and given in to temptation. Her reaction was not one of condemnation or even disappointment. It was thankfulness and, believe it or not, love. Jen actually responded by thanking me for being honest. We then talked about what had happened and what I could do in the future to keep it from happening again. Give your spouse that same opportunity. Be willing to open up and be vulnerable.

Your wife is not the enemy. Next to God, she is the greatest ally you can have. The real enemy is whatever is driving a wedge between you and God and you and your spouse. Take the time to sit down with your wife and talk about what might be driving the wedge right now. One of the greatest weapons you have in this battle is communication. But you have to first be willing to talk honestly with each other.

Remember, Your Wife Is Not God

A word of warning here: your wife may not exactly respond positively to your confession. It took Jen a long time to learn how not to respond with anger when it came to the porn addiction. Don't let that deter you. It's going to be hard, but it's worth it. If your wife hasn't caught you yet, it's only a matter of time.

My parents used to say, "It's always better to tell us about something rather than letting us find out about it on our own." I never believed them as a kid, but having gone through this process with Jen, I now know it's the truth.

Your wife will likely react out of her own hurt first. This is normal and expected. The reaction will probably be a mixture of shock, anger, and denial, much like the stages of grief.[4] You may need to prepare for some fireworks and I don't mean the celebratory kind. Love and pray through these stages. Forgive your spouse for anything she might say or do. Don't give in to your own anger and hurt and don't give up. It's a good idea not to assume a defensive posture. It's going to be a process, but it will get easier. The more you communicate with each other, the stronger your relationship will be. The trust *will* be rebuilt.

My parents received some sound advice from their folks, and they passed it on to me. Now I'm passing it on to you. It's Ephesians 4:26–27, "'Don't sin by letting anger control you.' Don't let the sun go down while you are still angry, for anger gives a foothold to the devil." In other words, don't go to bed angry. I haven't always followed this rule but I have found that when I did, I slept better and woke up feeling closer to Jen.

God chose your wife for you. He prepared her for you. He prepared you for your marriage. What God has joined together let nothing and no one put asunder, especially the fear of asking for forgiveness.

CHAPTER 12

Forgive and Forgive and Forgive

Above all, clothe yourselves with love, which binds us all together in perfect harmony.

Colossians 3:14

There's a saying "Hurt me once, shame on you. Hurt me twice, shame on me." We hope you don't subscribe to this theory because this would make reconciliation impossible—and reconciliation needs to happen daily (sometimes hourly) in a marriage.

Marriage to anyone, not just an addict, requires that we forgive multiple times for multiple offenses. Often, the same offenses need abundant grace to cover them.

How do we do this? Repenting means to turn away from sin and make changes for the better. But how do we forgive our spouses when we don't see those changes happening within them? How can we forgive when we aren't sure they are willing to fully leave that path of sin?

There once was a woman on a path of life filled with sexual sin. One day she was caught in the act of adultery and brought into the temple by the Pharisees as Jesus taught the people. Not only were the Pharisees interested in shaming the woman who broke the law, but they intended to trap Jesus. Either He would enforce the Jewish law (and break Roman law[1]) by executing her, or He would violate Jewish law by exonerating her.[2] Jesus' answer was brilliant: "All right, but let the one who has never sinned throw the first stone!" (John 8:7).

One by one, all the religious leaders dropped their stones to the ground and left. None of them were without sin. Jesus told her: "Go and sin no more" (8:11).

We don't know if this woman ever sinned again by committing adultery, but we do know that she sinned. We know this not because the Bible tells us, but because we know ourselves. "For everyone has sinned; we all fall short of God's glorious standard" (Romans 3:23).

Jesus' command wasn't to show her this was her last chance. It wasn't a final warning that she'd better make good because He spared her from brutal punishment. Rather, He told her to leave her life of sin because of the pain she was causing *herself* by engaging in a practice that leads to brokenness and separation from God. He told her to leave her old ways not as a threat, but as a path to love and a fulfilling life.

If Jesus were to find her a few weeks later in the same situation, would He do the same thing? Would He extend forgiveness, even though He had already forgiven her once? Yes!

If Jesus were to find you in front of the computer again looking at naked women after asking forgiveness for looking at porn yesterday, would He forgive you? Yes!

If Jesus were listening to your degrading comments and barbed remarks as you sit on your high horse about how you can't believe your husband would do this *again*, even though you had confessed to having a prideful heart last week, would He forgive you? Yes!

Does He expect us to forgive *each other* for the same sins we commit over and over again? Yes! Peter, Jesus' disciple, asked Him how often he should forgive his brother who sins against him (Matthew 18:21). Peter quite generously (he thought) suggested that we forgive seven times. Rabbinic code dictated that only three times was necessary. But that isn't sufficient for the standard of grace Jesus holds. He replied to Peter, "No, not seven times, but seventy times seven!" (18:22).

In case you're like me and can't do math quickly in your head, that's four hundred and ninety times. But the point isn't the actual number; it's the *vast scope* of the number in comparison to Peter's initial thought. Jesus' point is this: *Always forgive.*

I can't count the number of times Craig has said to me, "I can't live like this anymore!" in response to my controlling behavior or my sharp tongue. And how many times have I lamented the fact that Craig has fallen time after time into the clutches of porn? How many times have I wanted to bang my head against the wall, saying, "Why couldn't you have chosen differently?" The truth is, he says the same thing about me.

And yet, we are still married. And we are happy. A huge part of this is due to the fact that we have chosen to forgive.

We have *chosen*. Sometimes it has taken us longer to make that choice than it should have, but we got there some way or another. Along the journey of marriage, we had to learn that forgiveness, most of the time, doesn't start with a feeling; it starts with obedience to God. We know we must forgive because He has forgiven us time and time again (Colossians 3:13). We then put our faith in God that He will take our decision to walk toward forgiveness (i.e., leave grudges, resentment, bitterness, and anger behind) and bring it to fruition.

Moved by Compassion

As soon as Jesus told Peter he had far underestimated the amount of grace we are to extend to others, He illustrated His point with a parable. It's found in Matthew 18:23–35. Jesus compares God to a king who decided to balance his monetary accounts and find out who still owed him a debt. One of the debtors was brought to him, and since the man was unable to pay back the millions he owed the king, he was sentenced to be sold into slavery, along with the rest of his family. He would lose everything he owned.

Upon hearing this dreadful news, the debtor fell at the feet of the king and begged for time to pay it back, cent by cent. Jesus said, "And the lord of that slave *felt compassion* and released him and forgave him the debt" (Matthew 18:27 NASB, emphasis mine).

Directly after receiving this gift of incredible mercy (there is no mention of a "thank you"), the forgiven man set out to find a fellow servant who owed *him* a debt. When he found him, he did the exact opposite of what the king did for him and instead demanded instant payment for the few thousands owed him. Of course, this fellow servant begged in the same manner as the forgiven servant had, but instead of extending the same grace and mercy that he himself received, he had the man arrested and thrown in jail.

Clearly there is an immense difference between the way God is able to forgive and the way we are able to forgive. To what do we attribute this quantum difference? I think it is our humanness, our sinful nature. God doesn't have any baggage to get in the way of offering His children forgiveness. He is instantaneously moved by the *feeling of compassion* that motivates His effusive offer of forgiveness. His feelings and emotions are pure because He is without sin. There is only light and He knows no darkness.[3]

We, however, cannot rely on our feelings to prompt this life-giving, freeing response. Just typing this I realize how little I respond with a "thank you" to Jesus after He has granted me forgiveness from my own sin. How much am I like the forgiven but unforgiving servant when I contemplate whether or not my husband or anyone else who has hurt me deserves to be granted the same grace and mercy?

What sin gets in the way of our ability to feel compassion for others and then forgive them for their mistakes? Do any of these sins resonate with you: pride, bitterness, fear, the desire to self-protect against future hurts, self-pity, the need for "payback," distrust in God? All of these feelings and emotions hinder our ability to have compassion on the perpetrator. They act as blinders, inhibiting us from seeing that we are the same way. We are just like the object of our anger and hurt—imperfect and in need of grace.

Are You the Returning Prodigal or the Older Brother?

This is not the only example of God's compassion and our inability to muster it up on the first try. The same Greek word used for compassion *(splanchnizomai)* in the story from Matthew is also used in Jesus' parable of the prodigal son found in Luke 15. If you aren't familiar with it, the premise is that the younger of two sons asked his father for his full inheritance before his father was dead. This was a tremendous insult in that culture. It's as if the son said, "I wish you were already dead." The son then went out, partied hard, and ran out of money. He was left with no option but to return home as a slave for his father. Jesus tells the story, "While he was still a long way off, his father saw him and *felt compassion* for him, and ran and embraced him and kissed him" (Luke 15:20 NASB, emphasis mine).

This parable shows how much grace and mercy God extends to us. He is full of compassion and willingly forgives us when we do stupid and disastrous things. And, once again, we see how the human element quickly comes into play when the older brother makes his first appearance. We see him greet the situation the opposite way his father does. Full of pride and self-pity, he told his father:

> All these years I've slaved for you and never once refused to do a single thing you told me to. And in all that time you never gave me even one young goat for a feast with my friends. Yet when this son of yours comes back after squandering your money on prostitutes, you celebrate by killing the fattened calf! (Luke 15:29–30)

We human beings tend to set up a hierarchy of sins. Had the elder son ever sinned? Of course. He's human. But because he saw his sins juxtaposed with his brother's, he mistakenly saw them as ones easily dismissed.

As someone who has pretty much been a "good girl" all her life, I am the elder son incarnate. I have spent way too much time looking haughtily at people who have made "big" mistakes. This false hierarchy has blinded me from realizing that my very attitude of pride is causing me to sin just as greatly in the eyes of my Father as someone who has committed murder or had an affair.

Because I felt I needed to be forgiven little, I, therefore, forgave little. I had no room in my heart for compassion because I was already too full of myself. I chose to see my own hurt and self-indignation before I recognized my own faults. I chose to demand perfection before recognizing my own imperfection. And to prevent further damage to my heart, I sometimes chose to cloak myself in anger and push away my spouse or my friend or a complete stranger so that I didn't find myself vulnerable again.

Oh, but God! How many times have I hurt Him and He just welcomes me back? How many times have I struck out in my own legalism, and yet He still welcomes me home due to His grace and not my own careful rule following? I have no justification except through the eyes of Jesus. It is when I become aware of my own neediness and the sheer amount of compassion God has for me that I realize I have no reason—or right—to withhold forgiveness from anyone else.

I've grown enough to learn it doesn't matter if I'm right. I have been wrong. It doesn't matter if my anger is justified. My husband's anger has been justified, too. It doesn't matter if he's done it again. I've done it again, too. But all of these realizations are relatively new to me, while Craig has been living this way for most of his adult life.

Craig identifies much more with the prodigal son. Time and time again, he has left God and come back to God, only to leave again. Finally, he has chosen to stay, but not one time in his life did God ever reject him because of his abandonment, his poor choices, or his rebellious nature. Finding his way back home was intentional and each time he returned it was because he recognized he was desperately lost. He realized how far away his sin had taken him and he felt the weight of his remorse. Perhaps because using porn when you're a married Christian man seems to fit higher on the worldly scale of sins than say, having judgmental thoughts about the contents of another woman's grocery cart, he has a much deeper appreciation for God's forgiveness. Perhaps because he's made so many commitments to end his porn addiction but fallen short of the end goal, he's acutely aware of how long-suffering God is. As such, more often than not, he has been the one to forgive me without me asking, to let things go because he chose not to take them personally, and to let God deal with my squirrelly behavior instead of looking down his nose at me. Overarchingly, Craig's innate response toward me is more like God's simply because he has *recognized* God's compassion. He forgives much because he knows how much he has been forgiven.

We can't let ourselves be fooled by a hierarchy of sin. Sin is sin. All sin requires forgiveness. Until we recognize that we truly are all sinners, it will be incredibly difficult to be moved by compassion and prompted to forgive without first sifting through our own baggage and sinful desires.

What Does It Mean to Forgive?

Until I looked up the original Greek, I never would have imagined the primary root meaning of the word "forgive."[4] The Greek word used many times for the English word "forgive" is *aphiēmi*, which means "to leave." Jesus used this word when He told the story of the master and the debtor in Matthew 18. He used the same word while He hung on the cross, imploring His Father to "forgive them, for they don't know what they are doing" (Luke 23:34). What does He mean by "leave" when He uses the word "forgive?"

We gain a clue to the answer in Colossians 3 through the words of Paul when he tells us, "Now is the time *to get rid* of anger, rage, malicious behavior, slander, and dirty language" (Colossians 3:8, emphasis mine). The Greek word used here for the phrase "to get rid of" is *apotithemi*, which means to put off or aside or away. It has the same origin as *aphiēmi*. Therefore, when we forgive, we choose to leave behind our anger, rage, and maliciousness, and our slanderous, hurtful words. It is like we are taking off these things as though they are clothes. And as we leave those emotions behind, we can choose instead to "clothe [our]selves with love, which binds us all together in perfect harmony" (Colossians 3:14). Just as we learned to dress ourselves when we were children, we can practice clothing ourselves with love, which will enable us to feel compassion toward those who hurt us and forgive them. And when we clothe ourselves with love, we are clothing ourselves with God, for "God is love" (1 John 4:8).

And where do we leave our anger? At the foot of the cross. When it surges within us again, where do we put it? At the foot of the cross. Every time it comes, we lay it back down again. Inch by inch, time and time again, we give ourselves over to Him, asking Him to transform and change our hearts, to take away the anger and replace it with love. And we ask Him to fill that void with himself so that we may love and forgive as He does.

Forgiveness is not something we do by ourselves.

For you to discuss together:

1. What keeps you most from forgiving most often?

2. Do you find it hard to validate someone else's feeling because you feel like you would be admitting to being wrong?

3. How does viewing how God forgives you change how you might forgive others in the future? How can you continually be reminded of what He has done for you?

4. Do you need to ask your spouse for forgiveness? If so, for what?

PART 5

Breaking Old Cycles

CHAPTER 13

Men Have Cycles, Too

*Don't worry about anything; instead, pray
about everything. Tell God what you need, and
thank him for all he has done.*

Philippians 4:6

■ Her

I've lived much of my life on guard, steeling myself against
worst-case scenarios, sharp-barbs of criticism, and the unpredict-
ability of human behavior. If the fashion industry ever needed a
model for self-protective armor, they could have chosen me. I can
wear it with flair.

Part of self-protection is anticipating events so I can prepare
for them. As such, I have learned to be a suspicious person. I
believe if I assume the worst, I can somehow make the worst hurt
me less. This is not a fun way to live life.

Instead, I want to live so my heart is fully trusting in God.
I want to trade my armor for His armor.[1] I want to trust Him to
help me navigate tough situations as they arise instead of trying to
predict and control and manipulate. Of course I know it's not my
job to know everything, but I forget this, conveniently. Because to
let go of "not knowing" puts me in direct conflict with my desire
to try to keep life as safe and predictable as possible. I feel secure
when I have my little ducks quacking dutifully behind me in a

perfectly straight line. To let go is a risk. To stop suspecting Craig of using porn at every turn is a risk because I am tired of walking through the door and suffering the shock of seeing it all happen again. Porn is never a nice surprise.

Because I like things so orderly and safe, it is difficult for me to see what is going on, truly, with Craig, without this super-imposed layer of fear and anxiety, without suspecting the worst. Thus, when I look at him, my vision is sometimes clouded. I jump to conclusions. If I am afraid he is looking at porn, it must mean he *is* looking at porn. Sometimes it takes extraordinary effort not to become hypersensitive to his emotions and behavior.

I am learning to ask God for discernment first, to help me separate my own anxieties from what I think I am seeing in Craig. Let me give you an example, distinct from pornography.

As I write this, Craig is in Ireland on a business trip. This heightens my anxiety on multiple levels. There is his general safety for which I fear, the issues of being so far away, the lure of the secluded hotel room. On top of that, I have an irrational fear pulsating through my heart, seemingly with every heartbeat: I am terrified he is going to cheat on me.

Let me be the first to say this fear has no basis. Craig has never stepped out on me with a living, breathing human being in the same physical space. He is one of the most loyal, integrity-filled men I know. And I know it hurts him that I have this fear. "But he's in Ireland," I lament to God. "And he told me that before he met me, his dream was a red-headed, green-eyed girl with big boobs. There are a lot of those in Ireland, I surmise!"

When we've had a chance to FaceTime (visually talk with each other over the computer), I've made some snarky comments about where he had been and who he was with, which he lovingly took in stride (remember, he's quick to forgive). And as I say these catty words to him, I am filled with conflict. I know the truth—Craig is committed to fidelity—but I continue to speak out the lies . . . because I am afraid. I've put my fear out there so he knows it, but without being fully real about it. I haven't owned it. And I have done this because I didn't know why these doubts permeated me so deeply. But God knows I don't want to live out of fear. He knows I don't want to hurt my husband's feelings by always expecting the worst. And so, in the middle of chopping vegetables in my kitchen, He interrupted my thoughts and spoke this to my heart: *You think he will cheat on you because you don't feel worthy enough to have him. These fears are about you. They are not about him.*

I can't write these words without crying. Because it is true. And it makes me wonder how often I have accused him and not believed him, not because of his behavior, but because of the fallacies I have chosen to believe. Lies, fear, anxiety—they produce so much fog we can't discern even the outline of truth.

I don't think it's Craig's porn addiction that has me drowning in a sea of unworthiness. Certainly that has added to it, but the root goes back to years ago when I first picked up the notion that perfection was a requirement for worth. This is a lie that has succeeded in shattering me to pieces in various times of my life, but I don't want to project my own brokenness onto Craig. I want to know the truth in my heart and soul, the truth that says I am worthy because Jesus Christ died for me to give me forgiveness and unconditional love. I want to know the truth that I am worthy because God created me and gave me breath. I want to know the truth that I am worthy not because of what I do or what I look like, but because I simply am.

When my vision is unclouded by lies, I am able to see Craig's behavior more clearly. Unhindered by unnecessary fear, I have a better ability to see what is happening in our marriage, in Craig, and in myself without the distorting clouds of my self-protecting suspicion. When I tell God my worries and concerns and ask Him to give me wisdom and discernment, I allow Him to correct my vision. Allowing Him to restore my own brokenness means I can fulfill my role as a helper,[2] to be aware of potential pitfalls and warning signs so I can encourage, love, and communicate with Craig in a healthy way.

Porn addiction is cyclical and God can use me to help him break the cycle. However, I must first recognize my own unhealthy cycles, too.

His Cycle

Addictions all have triggers. Craig's primary trigger is stress. In the past, his cycle looked much like this:

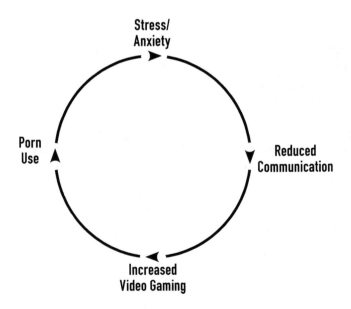

Stress/
Anxiety

Porn
Use

Reduced
Communication

Increased
Video Gaming

There was never one particular stressor that led him to begin this cycle. It could be stress from work, balancing commitments, family issues, or any combination of the above. Because Craig is an internal processor, meaning he generally thinks things through in his head, his first inclination is most often not to communicate with me or ask for help in taking things off his plate. He would stop sharing most anything, or brush me off with "Oh, it's just busy at work." After the kids were in bed, he might immediately sit down with his phone or computer instead of making space for communication with me. It's very easy to hide behind electronic devices.

Inside, he knew he needed something to give him release, but because he had not recognized the validity in talking things out with me, he would simply begin to disappear into video games. He would often take his frustrations out in that world and would find comfort in assuming an alter ego. But depending on the day, there was a chance things could go wrong in the game and he'd still be plagued with frustration and stress. Playing the video games never solved any problem. In fact, not finding success in this arena led right back into one of the reasons he gets stressed—he's afraid of failing or being rejected. Either way—whether he found success or failure video gaming, he was spending his time away from reality. The more time he spent in an alternative world, the "safer" he felt, the more convinced he became that avoidance was the answer. As such, his relationship with God, with me, and with his kids foundered. One cannot be fully present in two places at once.

Porn is quite similar in that it is an alternate (read here: *fantasy*) world. You can be whoever to whomever and satisfy whatever desires you have. The common thread between porn and video games is avoidance and retreat. We retreat from our "real life" to live out another however we want. When Craig started retreating into video games and spending excessive time engaged with that world, I realized he was ultra-susceptible to falling back into the world of pornography.

Even if he got away with engaging in porn, the activity gave way to a whole other level of stress, as porn brings shame and guilt to the user. Hence, the cyclical snare.

Your husband may not be into video games, but anything used excessively to escape reality can be a warning sign he's not coping well. It's easy to hide behind a myriad of things: overeating, drinking too much, exercising or working excessively. When we choose to indulge consistently in excessive behaviors, we risk shutting out the relationships God often uses to bring us back into fellowship with Him. Escaping into excessive video gaming was my red flag that things were too much for Craig to handle on his own and that he needed an outlet. It might be helpful to discuss with your spouse what escaping behaviors might come prior to or in conjunction with engaging with pornography.

One Cycle Begets Another

The stress/anxiety is the tangible start of the cycle; it's something he can feel. The cause of that stress/anxiety is also evident (increased workload, relationship problems). But the deeper insight into the cycle—what he can't always see—is the distrust in God that he shows when he doesn't allow Him to interrupt this unhealthy routine. When Craig chooses to live in stress and anxiety, he chooses not to trust God with his situation. And guess what? The same thing happens with me. If I see Craig caught in the clutches of the cycle (or think I'm seeing it) and react out of fear and my own brokenness, I choose not to trust God either. This starts my own cycle, pictured below.

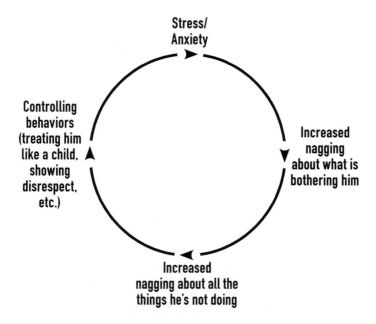

If I am spinning in my own cycle, there is no way I can productively help Craig out of his. The flip side is also true. If he is caught up in being the manager of his own stress instead of seeking God for help in carrying the load, there is no way he can help me combat my issues of fear and unworthiness. This is why it is so important to have a living, breathing relationship with God. As we discussed in chapter 6, we are a team, yoked as two oxen. We are designed to work together and help each other. If we are worried about protecting only ourselves, we cannot accomplish what God would have us do—either in our marriage or in the world around us.

So often God lays groundwork by softening our hearts to lead us out of these cycles. He allows certain circumstances, conversations, and random signs to prep our hearts for the message He wants us to receive. When the moment comes that we become cognizant of the triggers of our unhealthy cycles, we have to choose not only to see it but to *believe that God can do something about it.*

For example, prior to my revelation about my feelings of unworthiness in my marriage to Craig, I had spent the morning with a dear friend. I casually asked her about the new bike she had finally purchased. "I didn't sleep for a month after I bought it because it cost so much money," she confessed to me. The problem wasn't that she didn't have the money to spend. The problem wasn't that she didn't need a new bike. (Her old one was too small for her and was causing all sorts of kinks with her body.) She wasn't sleeping well because she didn't feel worthy enough to spend that much money on a bike, even though it would bring her much physical and mental wellbeing.

God got me thinking about worthiness the rest of that day. It kept rolling around in my head, and when my anxiety about why Craig hadn't called from Ireland that day peaked, the phantom fear of adultery and my own unworthiness clicked. In that moment, the cycle could begin to disintegrate because I had identified the trigger that launched the cyclical behavior.

Once we name our triggers, we can begin to allow God to disarm them of the power to set off our unhealthy behaviors. He can help us tear out the lies that keep us locked in, revealing to us truth that sinks into our minds *and* our hearts. We can begin to create a cycle based on trust instead of suspicion.

This is a process of unlearning and new learning. Since this revelation, I've still been snarky with Craig. Yes, the trigger has become more tangible, but the sense of unworthiness is still powerful. The fear still cloaks me, and I struggle to get out of the tangled mess. Every day I have to choose to believe the truth about what God says about me in order to keep unhealthy cycles at bay.

Just this morning I was reading in my devotional, *Jesus Calling*, and these words caused me to take a deep breath: "Approach each new day with desire to find Me."

I immediately had an image flash before my eyes. I was stuck in a room that was filled with thick, red, velvet curtains. I had to wade through all these drapes, pulling them back, weaving in and out, so I could find Jesus. Each one of these curtains was a layer of fear I needed to pull away, pull open to Light, so I could come out of my fears and see how He has made me worthy of every gift He has given me.

Sometimes I'll get trapped and tangled in the curtains. Sometimes you will too. But remember your desire to be free. And remember the way to freedom is this: the Truth (see John 8:32). And Jesus, who is the truth, will give you renewed vision so you can see it.

Red Flags and Warning Signs Are Not Symbols for Panic

It takes practice to remain untangled from lies and see situations without the lens of fear clouding everything. If I see warning signs that Craig is looking for a means to escape the current trials and tribulations of life, I must first do a heart check to make sure I have on the right glasses. Yes, red flags are a warning there could be trouble ahead, but I need to be in the right frame of mind so I can be the helper God has called me to be. I need Jesus' perspective and His reassurance at all times. Here are some steps I follow:

Ask God to help me see what is happening with His eyes. This spiritual process helps me discern if what I am seeing is a result of Craig's issues or my own. This looks like me sitting down in a quiet space and just being. If I'm not quiet, I can't look at things objectively or hear what He is trying to say to me. Reading God's

Word, because it is truth, helps me to establish whether what I am feeling or perceiving is truth. Remember, just because you feel something doesn't mean that it is a true representation of what is happening.

When in doubt, be honest. The last thing I want Craig to do is hide from me. Therefore, if I expect and desire honesty from him, I need to be able to give it *to* him. If I have a hard time pinpointing whether I am acting out of fear or genuine concern, I'll tell him what's going on inside my mind. I say to him something like, "I feel like you are pulling away from me and not talking to me as much. Am I reading too much into the situation? Can you share with me what's going on?" Sometimes, life just gets crazy and we don't make time to talk. I end up feeling disconnected and when that happens, my mind tends to wander in places it really shouldn't go. Saying something as simple as this lets Craig know that I'm yearning to connect and trying not to jump to conclusions or make accusatory remarks.

Be gentle. If Craig is stressed and looking for comfort, he's not going to turn to me if I've been harping on him about things. I want to provide an encouraging, safe place for him. I want to withhold judgment and welcome authenticity. Sometimes it's a great battle to get to a place of gentleness when I'm afraid of the choices he will make. But my prayer is that with time and practice, I will get there.

Remember to surrender and pray. When there is trouble ahead and I see Craig not making the best choices, it is easy for me to want to jump in and bail him out myself. But I cannot do this because it is not my job. It's Craig's job to submit to Jesus and Jesus' job to bring that process to fruition. It does no use to try to protect myself and Craig from every foreseeable trial. Jesus tells us, "Here on earth you will have many trials and sorrows. But take heart, because I have overcome the world" (John 16:33). I have to trust in His overcoming and His power to redeem all things.

God Is Enough

I have a thirst to truly believe I am worthy. I have a hunger for a marriage that is whole, healthy, and everything God intended it to be. But these cannot be what drive me every day. If they were, I would remain a woman who looks to that which is in this world for validation and one who feels an intense need to control her every move (and everyone else's, too). Instead, I must thirst and hunger for God. He is the One who can be my refuge, a safe place when I am confused, broken, and inflicted with cloudy vision.

> O God, you are my God;
> I earnestly search for you.
> My soul thirsts for you;
> my whole body longs for you
> in this parched and weary land
> where there is no water. (Psalm 63:1)

This world likes to live by what it can see. Sitting and just being with God can feel like a foreign concept, one that takes too much time, and is too open-ended. There isn't a script to follow. But it is life changing. It's a new beginning. It's a surrender that is the only way to true peace. So, if you have a tight hold on the reins of your marriage or your husband—if you are afraid that if you let go, everything will fall apart—know that it just might. But God can put it and you and him back together in a way you never imagined. Let's get quiet together now. He will speak. He will listen. It just begins with being still and opening our hands.

CHAPTER 14

Plugged in Offline

Search for the Lᴏʀᴅ and for his strength; continually seek him.

1 Chronicles 16:11

◼ Him

I picked up my phone and sent a text to Jen: "Please pray. I'm feeling tempted." In the moment, it was so hard to do. It would have been so much easier to slip back into the old behavior patterns. But at that moment I realized that temptation and sin are temporary. The guilt and shame of falling into sin stick around a lot longer.

At the time, Jen and the girls were at a friend's dance recital and I had the house to myself. So there I was, on the couch, writing and minding my own business when suddenly, the temptation came. "Just take a quick look. It's okay. No one is around. No one will know." It was the all-too-familiar voice of temptation and I was faced with a choice.

It's not too often that I'm alone in the house. I had an upcoming trip, and Jen and I had discussed strategies I could use while I was away. So the ideas were fresh, and I knew that Jen would come back home and ask me, "So, how did it go?" The "it," of course, was my problem with pornography.

I asked myself, *Why put yourself in a situation where you will want to lie to her?* Instead, I thought, *Why not reach out to her and ask for help?* God reminded me that to be successful, I needed to allow others to help me. At that moment, I needed to engage with Jen, my partner, my wife. So I picked up the phone and sent the text.

Several minutes passed with no response from Jen, and I grew nervous. Was she mad? Did I totally freak her out? Would she want to immediately leave the dance recital and come home? With each second ticking, my anxiety level increased. Just as I was about to send a follow-up text, the response came: "Praying."

A sense of relief washed over me. It had worked! Jen wasn't mad. Instead she was engaged and helping me fight! I began to relax. I could imagine her reaching out to God and asking Him to help me. Then, I was able to focus my attention back on my work. I actually sensed her prayers, and the desire evaporated. It was a victory—a sweet, awesome victory.

Yet I have not always been successful. Why was this particular instance significant? It was the first time I can remember reaching out to Jen in the moment of temptation and asking for help. I finally admitted to myself that I could not overcome each temptation based on my own willpower alone. I cannot simply rely on myself. I cannot trust my own strength and force of will to keep me from danger. Proverbs 3:5–6 tells us:

> Trust in the LORD with all your heart;
>> do not depend on your own understanding.
> Seek his will in all you do,
>> and he will show you which path to take.

We have to rely on God and His power. Our first step is to recognize and admit that we are powerless to overcome our own addiction to pornography. This acceptance allows us the freedom to engage with other people such as our spouse, pastor, and close friends that we trust. God loves us and wants us to be in relationship with Him and with our people. He will use these relationships to help us through our struggles, and He will use us to help others as well. This book you're reading is a prime example of that. Don't be anxious about the future. Instead, let's focus our attention and intentions on God, His will, and His work.

Tackling Temptation Head On

For me, temptation to engage with pornography can come on suddenly or it can grow incrementally. But once it starts, I get a sinking feeling in my stomach. The intensity can range from a small itch to an overpowering compulsion. My mind fills up with all kinds of images from the past, or perhaps it's instigated by the present moment. I could pass a scantily clad woman at the grocery store and the next thing I know, my mind is filled with flashbacks to a movie I used to watch or a website I would browse. All the while the same messages keep playing in my head: "Scratch the itch. It's okay. Nobody will know. It's no big deal. Everyone does it." Does any of this sound familiar?

During the fight against temptation, my emotional state can vary from panic to frustration. I'm fearful of failing. I'm worried about what will happen if I do fail. I'm stressed about figuring out why I'm still struggling. And then sometimes I get angry—angry that I'm so weak and unable to defeat this enemy and win the battle. Yet in the midst of my turmoil I hear God speak to me, "Craig, you have a choice. You always have a choice."

Ironically, the very nature of the temptation shows me how good God is. When the draw of temptation comes and I find myself walking toward the computer, or reaching for the TV remote, or picking up my phone or tablet, I will hear God's voice gently reminding me, "Craig, you have a choice. You always have a choice."

So now we come to the heart of the issue: you and sin. What do you picture when you think about sin? How do you feel about it? It is dark? Seductive? Evil? Overpowering? When I'm facing sin, I feel the freedom and responsibility of choice. God, in His infinite wisdom, has given you and me the power to choose Him or sin when faced with temptation. The power of choice is one of His greatest gifts. It makes us fully human, and image bearers of God.

I don't like being told what to do. I prefer to be involved in discussing the options and provided with a choice. And that is exactly what God offers us. He wants us to talk to Him to pour out our struggles, our hopes, and our desires. He wants us to listen to Him and His words as they gently guide us to the right choice. But the choice is ours to make. He won't make it for us.

I have come to discover that in my brokenness I am unable to make the correct choice when I rely on myself. My wife can certainly help me, but it is only by relying on God and His power that I can be successful.

Before I left for my trip, Jen gave me a sheet of reminders and strategies to help me fight temptation. She knows that when I'm faced with temptation, especially in an empty hotel room, I'm more likely to reach for a resource if it's right in front of me. I've included the points below along with my commentary.

You are strong when you depend on the Lord. Paul talks about the "thorn" in his side in 2 Corinthians 12:6–10:

> If I wanted to boast, I would be no fool in doing so, because I would be telling the truth. But I won't do it,

because I don't want anyone to give me credit beyond what they can see in my life or hear in my message, even though I have received such wonderful revelations from God. So to keep me from becoming proud, I was given a thorn in my flesh, a messenger from Satan to torment me and keep me from becoming proud. Three different times I begged the Lord to take it away. Each time he said, "My grace is all you need. My power works best in weakness." So now I am glad to boast about my weaknesses, so that the power of Christ can work through me. That's why I take pleasure in my weaknesses, and in the insults, hardships, persecutions, and troubles that I suffer for Christ. For when I am weak, then I am strong.

I have often felt that my addiction to pornography is much like the thorn Paul mentioned. I have been kept humble by my weakness. It has allowed to me to be understanding and compassionate with others in their struggles with sin. It has strengthened my relationship with my wife and my God. If I could live a perfect life on my own, there would be no need for me to have a deep and meaningful relationship with God or my wife. Dealing with the temptation allows me to stay tethered tightly to the power and love that is from God. And I no longer want to live a life devoid of this power and love.

He loves you and can bring you real *joy and freedom.* Isn't this what we really want? Isn't this what we are seeking? Joy and freedom! Not only can God provide both, but He *wants* to! This took me a long time to figure out and accept. God *wants* to bring me joy and freedom. No longer do I think of freedom as doing what I want to do. True freedom is living the life God has planned for me, a life free of guilt and shame. He wants the same for you.

Now, what about some tangible steps you can take embrace God's help to escape pornography and stay engaged with real life? Keep in mind, God may use some of these things and not others in order to specifically help you. In my experience, some men have experienced success by attending support groups, while other men have not. The key to figuring out what works for you is obedience. How is God asking you to participate in your recovery? I believe the source of freedom is always Jesus, but He can use programs and people to help us. But these are simply tools to foster a deeper relationship with Him. They are not the cure.

I imagine it much like a chandelier. The lights on the chandelier are like the resources God can use to help you overcome temptation. However, if they are not attached to the source of electricity, they will have no power. It is God who gives the resources power, just like electricity brings light to the chandelier. If you put your trust in the light bulb instead of the power source, you will face disappointment. As you read the following list, be open to God's nudge to see if He's pointing out something that can help you.

- *Pray first. Ask for His presence to surround and fill you.* You've got to surrender. Stop fighting alone. The first call for reinforcements should be to God. Paul writes, "The temptations in your life are no different from what others experience. And God is faithful. He will not allow the temptation to be more than you can stand. When you are tempted, he will show you a way out so that you can endure" (1 Corinthians 10:13).

- *Conduct a quick self-check.* What's going on in your life at that moment? Are you stressed? Are you lonely? Are you looking for comfort? James writes, "Temptation comes

from our own desires, which entice us and drag us away"
(1:14). Being aware of our needs and learning how to fill
them will empower us to fill them with things that are beneficial instead of detrimental.

- *Call/text your spouse.* You need to be united with your wife
in this fight. Next to God, she is your greatest ally. She is
the one who will stand with you when all others abandon
you. Cling to that and then claim it.

- *Call/text an accountability partner.* I have a couple of men
with whom I have shared my struggle and can rely on to
pray for me. God might call you to have an accountability
partner. This is a friend you can be completely honest with
and trust to keep your confidence. Having an accountability partner has helped me out of some temptation troubles.
God wants us to work with and help each other. However,
an accountability partner isn't someone who asks scripted
questions each week so you can lie to him. He isn't someone with a prying interest in the dark corners of your life.
He isn't someone with an unhealthy need to be exhibition-
istic about his own dark secrets. An accountability partner
is a brother who understands and accepts your struggles,
who is with you in the fight, and who wants to know how
to pray at that particular time. You might also investigate
local or online support groups.

- *Go outside.* Instead of seeking out fake beauty, experience
true beauty in God's creation. Scripture is full of references
to God's beauty and hand in nature. Job, in his poetic
defense to his "friends," put it this way:

But ask the animals, and they will teach you,
or the birds in the sky, and they will tell you;
   or speak to the earth, and it will teach you,
   or let the fish in the sea inform you.
Which of all these does not know
   that the hand of the LORD has done this? (Job 12:7–9 NIV)

- *Pray with thanksgiving. Think of what He's given you.* I look at my life and God has blessed me with abundance. I have a beautiful, loving wife, fantastic kids who are much smarter than I was at their age, wonderful friends and family who are completely supportive. Why would I seek anything else? I have to remind myself that God is my sole provider and the source of my life. I thank Him for everything, good and bad.

- *Exercise.* A study conducted in 1999 examined the effects of exercise on depression. One group was given an exercise program, the second was given Zoloft (an antidepressant), and the third received both. At the conclusion of the study, the groups scored almost the same results on the depression tests! Even in a follow-up, those who exercised were less likely to relapse into depression. If one of your triggers is stress or depression, exercise is a great option. The health benefits don't hurt either.

- *Think of any upcoming event that you might be looking forward to.* For me, this was an anniversary trip with Jen. I recommend you think about something involving your family (preferably your spouse). Doing this helps focus your mind and attention to your support network. These are the folks who love you and are praying for you. They want you to be successful. With God's help, you will be.

We all have the power of choice. God in His infinite wisdom blessed us with this tremendous gift. Through my struggles with porn I have learned that I can either choose to engage with porn or I can choose to engage with God. All of you have that same choice as well. When you next face temptation, what will you choose?

"As for me and my family, we will serve the LORD" (Joshua 24:15).

CHAPTER 15

It's Not Always Linear

Simon Peter replied, "Lord, to whom would we go? You have the words that give eternal life."

John 6:68

We live our lives marked by time on a calendar that follows a sequence of days, yet it's clear that nothing follows a perfectly straight line. Events, people, and actions are never as expected. The stock market drops; we get surprise bonuses on our paychecks. There are fever spikes, a brief return to normal, and then another unexpected resurgence of heat as our bodies kill the last few remnants of a virus. There are deaths at early ages, heat waves during winter (at least in Texas), and one-hit wonders who make it big on the pop charts. The only sure thing that moves in one direction is this: my children keep getting taller.

Even this won't last forever. Children stop growing after a time. They'll remain the same height for many years, and then start heading the other direction.

Instead of straight lines, the world seems to work more in cycles. We have life cycles, weather cycles, lunar cycles. Porn addiction fits right in to this world of cycles. All sin does. We sin, we repent, we receive forgiveness, and then we sin again. We are human. God expects this. But this is not just another mundane, predictable cycle. There is another powerful dimension at work here—our spiritual growth. And unlike our children's physical growth, this does not have to stop. Nor does it ever have to diminish.

Many times when we struggle with the same sin over and over, we feel we consistently return to square one or go backward. But this is one-dimensional thinking. We don't see how each time we return, we are engaging again with God. And when we do this, He gets into our hearts. He churns up the soil, loosens up the hard-packed dirt, pulls a weed or two. He adds His truth and plants some seeds. Our encounters with God never leave us unchanged. We may not recognize all He does within us, but it doesn't mean transformation isn't happening. *The Message* puts it this way, "Instead, fix your attention on God. You'll be changed from the inside out" (Romans 12:2). When we talk to Him, look for Him, read His Word, repent, ask questions, share our emotions (even our anger), we are changed by His presence, no matter if we feel the change or not.

Messing Up in the World

We all sin. But how do we deal with our sin? What messages do we take as truth but are really lies? This fallen world sends us all kinds of messages when we fall short. We hear things like, *"You can only mess up so much and then you become unworthy," "Forward momentum is all there is,"* and *"Grace is limited."* Messages like, *"Success must be earned"* and *"You can only rely on yourself"* clog our brains. And one of the biggest lies: *"If you mess up, you'd better fix it."*

If we let these words echo loudly in the recesses of our hearts, we won't be able to hear God's truth. In her book *So Long, Insecurity*, Beth Moore says, "We're going to have to let truth scream louder to our souls than the lies that have infected us."[1] God's truth says that when we find ourselves in trouble, be it crisis, sin, confusion, or failure, that we can turn to Him. In Hebrews, we find these words that help us break the cycle of self-dependence and limited mercy:

> This High Priest of ours understands our weaknesses, for
> he faced all of the same testings we do, yet he did not sin.
> So let us come boldly to the throne of our gracious God.
> There we will receive his mercy, and we will find grace to
> help us when we need it most. (Hebrews 4:15–16)

God knows we need Him. *We* just need to know that we need Him. We will never use up all His grace and mercy. It does not come from a well that threatens to run dry. We don't have to prove our worth in order to receive help. Psalm 46:1 says, "God is our refuge and strength, *always ready to help* in times of trouble (emphasis mine). God is ready to help at any point in our lives—when temptation comes, after we've fallen into temptation, when we've resisted temptation. And He is ready to help because it means engaging with His children. Remember, God is all about relationship.

We will never be able to be fully free of the cycle of sin on this earth because we live in a fallen world. Even if God helps us to conquer addictions to porn and control, there will be other sins. But we *can* break the cycle of listening to the world's advice instead of scriptural truth. We can allow God to turn our sin into opportunities for great spiritual growth. How do we do this?

What's in Your Toolbox?

While we are guilty of different offenses, Craig and I both suffer from the affliction of self-reliance. Both of us were raised in good churches, so we always knew about the need to repent of our sins and ask for forgiveness. But what neither of us really knew is that we need a continual relationship with God so we would not remain afflicted by the same sin. We approach God on His throne of grace, but we forget that He doesn't just sit there. He longs to walk *with* us.

In our self-reliant nature, after being granted forgiveness, we would turn from the throne, walk back down the path which we came, and try, with our own ability and strength, to keep from coming back to have to ask for forgiveness again. If I was struggling with my anger, I might resolve to not yell, determined to take lots of deep breaths when things didn't happen like I planned. If Craig engaged with porn, he might resolve to go back to counseling or join a support group. None of these things are bad. They can be good strategies that help us to deal with temptation and sin. But this is the key: These tools have to be used in conjunction with God.

If we walk away alone, not holding onto the hand of God, it is so easy to convince ourselves we can do it on our own. And then, when we fail, we are an easy target for lies. Here's the truth: It's so easy to fall back into old traps and bad habits, no matter how hard we try to stay away from them. It's so easy not to believe the truth of God's Word that He always wants us to return to Him. Yet Jesus says, "The Spirit alone gives eternal life. Human effort accomplishes nothing. And the very words I have spoken to you are spirit and life" (John 6:63).

Craig and I wonder: Are you trying to break this cycle of porn addiction, control addiction, or any other addiction by yourself? And if so, who is in charge of the repair? What measure of success are you having? Would you be willing to see if God's help in times of trouble might bring your more freedom? More growth? More satisfaction with the person God created you to be?

A comparison to the ancient Israelites can be helpful here, even if it isn't fun. In Isaiah 30, we find the Israelites fighting to protect themselves. The Assyrians (a neighboring power) threatened to run them out of town, destroy their community, and take over their land. But instead of turning to God for help, the Israelites turned to Egypt, a country whose power was waning. It was also a country that had enslaved them for centuries. For some reason, the Israelites thought seeking them out for refuge and relief was a brilliant idea.

Sometimes we humans can do such stupid things, can't we? We can't get past our immediate needs and worldview, and so we grasp at anything we think might offer tangible relief. Often in our lives, we don't allow God room to become tangible to us. And so, we look into our worldly toolbox. We make plans and alliances. We build walls, construct rules, create hiding places. We do things to make us feel better about ourselves, to prove ourselves worthy. We try to excel in other areas in a futile effort to hide our failures. Or we just shrivel up and label ourselves "of no use." The worldly toolbox consists of many labels that can rob us of our dignity, purpose, and fulfillment.

God speaks to the Israelites as they chase after the empty power of the Egyptians:

> This is what the Sovereign LORD,
> the Holy One of Israel, says:
> "Only in returning to me
> and resting in me will you be saved.
> In quietness and confidence is your strength."
> (Isaiah 30:15)

The tools in God's toolbox are much different. There is no scheming. There is no striving. There are no outside alliances. But what is it in this box that leads us away from trouble?

God's Tools

It boggles my mind that God's tools are things like *returning* to Him, *resting, quietness,* and *confidence.* The first three things really blow me away because they are the opposite of how I see the world work every day. I truly believed that hard work, striving, and planning were the only ways to make Craig and me better people (or to save our marriage). I more clearly understand the concept of confidence because the world expects us to have some measure of this in ourselves. Ah, but this is where careful study leads us to uncover the design and purpose of this tool. This is not a confidence we find in ourselves. This is a confidence in God.

The original Hebrew word for "confidence" in Isaiah 30:15 is *betach.* This exact form is only used in this verse. However, if we trace it back to the primary root word, we find the meaning to be equal to "trust." It literally means to go quickly to refuge.[2] If we can get *quiet,* tuning out the pressures, lies, and ways of the world, we can run to Him boldly, for He is a trustworthy refuge who will give us the strength we need to help us through our crisis, our sin, and trouble. And here is the crucial point: He never asks us to leave Him as a refuge. It is only with Him and through Him that we can we stay equipped to fight the lies and live in the fullness He intends for us.

But so often we don't seek God as a refuge. We continue to do life on our own and try to get ourselves out of trouble. We ignore God and neglect the things He uses to bring life and energy to our tired souls. How many times has God tried to show me safe people who can speak encouragement to me, and yet, I decide to cover up my pain? How many times has God put godly men in Craig's path and he has chosen to talk about cars and history and computers, instead of his heart? How many times have both of us heard the call to "be still," but instead we fill our lives with rushing and busyness and silly time-wasters? And the words God tells the Israelites are words that are true for us, too. At the close of verse 15, we read: "But you would have none of it." This kills my heart every single time. All too often, I would also "have none of it." None of the rest, none of the stillness, none of the confidence.

Isaiah goes on in verse 16 to explain that instead of seeking the God who performed miracles to save them from the Egyptians, they were depending on Egypt because they could give them "swift horses for riding into battle." How measly is this compared to the power of God *who parted a sea* to help the Israelites get away from slavery? How meager are my ways to strengthen and uphold myself when I feel ill-equipped to face the trouble of the world? I don't ask a neighboring country for horses, but I begin to turn to the world's way of measuring things in order to strengthen me. I start counting stats on my blog traffic. I try to find order by having a neat, clean house. I try to manage my weight obsessively. I take refuge in having enough money in the bank to go on a small shopping spree. Craig chooses video games or food or just an "ignorance is bliss" attitude.

Even though these things may bolster our moods for a moment, they do nothing to save us from the trouble that causes us to run to them in the first place. They do nothing to quiet our souls, quell our worry, or fill our emptiness, even though we believe in the moment that they will bring us peace, self-esteem, security, acclamation, or a sense of being loved. How easy it is to believe lies!

At some point, we have all been guilty of striking out on our own, whether that means trying to fix the problem by ourselves or ignoring it. When we finally realize we have a God who is always for us, always offering the tools we need, always loving us despite ourselves, we might find ourselves sounding like the apostle Peter. In John 6 some of the disciples had a hard time understanding the message Jesus was conveying, and so they deserted Him.[3] Jesus turned to the twelve apostles to ask them if they, too, will leave.

Peter replied: "Lord, to whom would we go? You have the words that give eternal life. We believe, and we know you are the Holy One of God" (John 6:68–69). Perhaps Peter had come to the end of himself, and all he could see was Jesus. Perhaps Peter had sought refuge in the world many times over, but now he found a place that was forever trustworthy and true. How many times have I come to the same conclusion?

The Cycle of Grace

I love the fact that it is Peter who says this to Jesus. It's the same Peter who later denies Jesus three times after He has been arrested.[4] The same Peter whom Jesus asks three times if he loves Him.[5] Peter professes he would never leave, and yet, because of his humanness, he does. It happens to all of us. But each time Peter fell short, Jesus met him again. He talked with him. He sought him out. He gave him more and more responsibility to carry out His word and His mission. This is the cycle of grace.

Every time we fall short and return to God, we rest in His love and forgiveness. And we allow Him to rebuild us with His strength. We allow Him to plant more scriptural truths in our hearts and weed out the world's lies. We remember that if He is for us, who can really stand against us?[6] Do we want to stand before God at the end of the day and hear that we "would have none of it"—none of the rest, none of the quietness, none of the returning, none of the confidence?

Satan wants to trick you into making you feel bad about coming back to God after you have messed up. He is very good at obscuring our internal growth or prompting us to believe growth isn't happening in our spouse. How often have I believed the lie that since I could not "see" anything happening in Craig, he must not be growing in His walk with the Lord? Often, I promise. But maybe I'm looking for the wrong thing. Or looking with the wrong eyes.

One day as I walked past our kitchen sink, I noticed the avocado seed I had left sitting in water for about three weeks. (That's how you get them to sprout.) I saw none of the expected growth—no roots, no sprouts on the outside. Yet, when I looked closely at the pit *resting* in the cool water, I noticed some cracking. The hard shell had lines that seemed to be growing deeper as it sat in the sun and absorbed the light and water. And this is growth, too. It amazes me what can come forth when my husband and I sit and absorb light and drink from the Living Water.[7] Even if the world judges us for waiting and trusting, we are learning to measure ourselves and each other, by the standard of endless grace.

For you to discuss together:

1. Read Isaiah 30:15–16:

> This is what the Sovereign Lord,
> the Holy One of Israel, says:

"Only in returning to me
and resting in me will you be saved.
In quietness and confidence is your strength.
But you would have none of it.
You said, 'No, we will get our help from Egypt.
They will give us swift horses for riding into battle.'
But the only swiftness you are going to see
is the swiftness of your enemies chasing you!"

2. The Israelites turned to Egypt to find help in their time of trouble. Both of you, individually, complete these sentences and share:

- I said, "No, I will get my help from _____."
  (To what do you turn when you feel you are in the midst of trouble?)

- In the moment, I think these things will give me

  _____.

3. When you turn to something else in times of trouble, what are you rejecting? What gifts do you think He wants to give you, but of which you would have none?

4. You may not be seeing growth in your spouse right now, but spend a moment in prayer together, asking God to help you see him/her with His eyes. Then, start looking for the cracking of the hard shell, no matter how fine the lines may be. And even if you still can't see them, commit to pray for your own growth and that your spouse will grow near to God.

PART 6

Winning the Battle

CHAPTER 16

Lean On Me

For where two or three gather together as my followers, I am there among them.

Matthew 18:20

◼ Her

I've had a lot of opportunities to share with friends and those curious to know about this book. But even though I've now said "porn addiction" more times than I can count, there are still moments when I pause before I speak, when I wonder if it's really okay that I'm sharing a very deep part of our marriage. The truth is, more people are talking about their struggles with this kind of addiction. It's becoming less taboo. Light begins to crack through the darkness. But there is still a sense of shame and trepidation in *my* heart at times. Thoughts of *Will you judge me? Will you think twice about the man I married?* cloud my mind. It can take a long time to shake the shame.

The good news: It does get easier every time I am honest. In the beginning of this process, I often let shame clamp my mouth shut or perhaps utter the only words my emotional self would permit: "It's a book about marriage." But when I am honest, an amazing thing happens: People sigh with relief. And then they go on to utter things like this:

"It's such a big problem."

"This is so needed."

"I am so glad you and your husband are talking about this."

"How much longer until the book comes out? I have people who need it yesterday."

And sometimes, this sharing elicits tears in the eyes of the woman listening to my story. She cries because there is relief in finding a friend who has walked a similar road. Hope dawns when you realize you're not the only one.

As Craig and I share this journey, people have asked hard questions. They range from "What about your kids?" to "What if people at Craig's work find out?" or the simplest one, "Don't you care how people will perceive you?"

It comes down to weighing the risks. And as a girl who has sought the world's approval her whole life, it is a real risk that people might look down on us for admitting this or for even having this problem in the first place. But we fully believe we are called to share our story. And deeper still, we feel called to be real to this world, to no longer hide behind a cloak of shame, not to let others sit in the darkness, and to declare to the world that God is hope and light and can save us from anything we are willing to surrender to Him.

So, yes, there is risk, but the reward is greater. The Bible says, "But we have this treasure in jars of clay to show that this all-surpassing power is from God and not from us" (2 Corinthians 4:7 NIV). I love how Jennie Allen, Bible teacher and the author of *Chase*, expounds on this verse. She writes:

> Christ's Spirit is this treasure inside of our broken lives,
> in us, moving and working in powerful and unique ways.

Imperfect jars of clay each shaped uniquely to hold the Spirit of God for different purposes, each with unique marks and cracks and broken places. And through those spaces God shines out. The shameful places are torn down and become the places that are most useful to God.[1]

We have a choice, wives. We have a choice to give power to our shame or allow God to give power to our lives. We want God's gift of freedom to be for many more beyond ourselves. From the beginning, both of us have said we would be grateful for the opportunity to write this book, even if the contract fell through. And we have said this because of what God has done in us as individuals and as a couple. It is worth going through the hard places for the salvation of our marriage. But there is also tremendous blessing when we look beyond our own little lives and live for something greater. *And we don't have to wait until we feel perfectly healed before we start talking about it.*

It is an honor to be a warrior for God and speak out His message. It's an honor to fight against shame. It's an honor to fight against the darkness when God calls us to do so. And it's an honor to be used by God, *even when we still are broken vessels.*

When to Share, What to Say

Craig and I have seen remarkable things happen when we have shared our brokenness with those around us. There is value in speaking out about the sinful traps into which we fall. I am not just talking about getting up in front of five hundred people and sharing my testimony. When I say "speaking out," I am talking about something as little as telling my best friend. Yes, we are sharing our story on a large scale, but there were hundreds of times we shared with friends because we were desperately in need of rescue. There is value in seeking help, whether that is a counselor or a friendly, safe shoulder on which to cry. There is value in sharing where we are presently, without being able to tie everything up with a bow. We are meant to live in community. God designed us so that we would have relationships that draw us further into relationship with Him.

Recently I spoke to a girlfriend who was just getting used to the idea of sharing her burdens with a few close friends. Her whole life she had been programmed to believe she wasn't supposed to rely on anyone except herself. Yet at the same time, she felt compelled to help other friends who needed someone to shoulder their trials.

I believe God put in us this innate desire to help each other, but often, when we are the ones in need, we convince ourselves that perhaps we should just carry on alone. We tell ourselves that no one else could withstand the weight. We think our burden to be too much and people are too busy with their own issues and problems. We push aside the notion of asking for help because we are afraid we might be judged, looked down upon, invalidated, or disbelieved.

But in Galatians we find this: "Share each other's burdens, and in this way obey the law of Christ" (6:2). The law of Christ is love! When we carry each other's burdens and give someone else the opportunity to carry ours, we are helping each other to walk in obedience to Him. The Greek word for "burdens" here is *baros*, which is translated as "weight" or "hardship." Truthfully, there are tremendously difficult things in this life that we are not designed to carry by ourselves and if we do, we will bring physical, emotional, and spiritual injury to ourselves. You wouldn't try to pick up a two-ton boulder by yourself. Why would you carry your husband's porn addiction by yourself? You were not made to hoist this on your shoulders and figure it all out on your own. If you don't rely on a community of support, the lies, shame, and heartache will take its toll on you emotionally, physically, and spiritually. And you will miss out on how God wants to bless you through His people.

Two additional verses from Galatians 6 merit our attention. Verses 4–5 say, "Each one should test their own actions. Then they can take pride in themselves alone, without comparing themselves to someone else, for each one should carry their own load" (NIV). The word "load" in verse five is not synonymous with the word "burden" in verse two. Instead, the Greek translation of "load" is *phortion*. It is same word that Jesus uses in Matthew, when He says, "For my yoke is easy to bear, and the burden I give you is light" (11:30). The load we are to carry as signified by this verse is proportional to how God designed us. It is like a backpack that fits easily on our shoulders, not a crushing boulder that threatens to buckle our knees and crush our souls.

God designed us to need to share our hardships. But there is one thing we must contemplate before we ask for help regarding this particular burden: When you share your heart as a wife who knows her husband is struggling with porn addiction, you are also sharing your husband's heart, too. Remember, he most likely is carrying a burden of shame and embarrassment. Or perhaps he has convinced himself porn isn't wrong and he doesn't want you to contradict his way of thinking, saying he is wrong to your friends. On some level, you need to keep him covered and respect his process. But this does not negate your need for an outlet, a trusted person who can help you see beyond what you see, who can encourage you, and build you up. You need someone who will remind you of God's truth.

Below you will see some guidelines Craig and I use before we share anything about the porn addiction, whether it's with a friend, a group, or online.

1. Tell your spouse exactly *what* you want to share.

2. Tell your spouse *why* you want to share it.

3. Tell your spouse *with whom* you are going to share the information.

If your husband doesn't feel comfortable with you telling anyone, seeing a licensed therapist, counselor, or priest/pastor may be the best option. They are bound by confidentiality agreements.

The Armor of God

We all have different reasons for sharing the hard parts of our lives. When we share about our brokenness and hurts caused by others, it's important to take stock of why we want to share. Honestly, we don't want to share so our friends will see our husbands as the evil bad guys (well, we might, but that's not a very edifying reason to share). The most beneficial aspects to my sharing with my friends when I was hurting because of Craig's porn use was that they reminded me of these key points:

- Craig's addiction was not related to how I looked.

- Craig's addiction was not a problem I could solve or control.

- It was okay to feel hurt, but I could also press through the hurt toward forgiveness.

- God can redeem all things, even porn addiction.

The truth is, though, even our closest friends can say things that aren't beneficial to our marriages or our hearts. How do we know if what they are saying is right for us? How do we know if we should heed their words or toss them? Let's face it—most women love to give advice. And we love to support our friends. Here are some guidelines to keep in mind.

(If you don't have a support network of people you can trust, ask God to send you one. He wouldn't ask you to live in a community and then not provide one for you. If you do have a network, pray and ask God to show you who within that group would be a good person to share with first.)

Before you meet to share with someone, whether it is the first time or the one-hundredth, don't forget to accessorize correctly. This isn't actual clothing, but rather, the armor of God. Don't laugh. If you were raised in the church, you might have grown up singing songs about being in the Lord's Army and pretending to be warriors dressed for battle, but the armor of God isn't just for Sunday school classes and it's not just for kids. In Ephesians 6:11, Paul writes, "Put on all of God's armor so that you will be able to stand firm against all strategies of the devil." Believe me, the devil has lots of strategies and he will try to come against anything you want to do that will lead to the salvation of your marriage and freedom for your husband. Sharing sins brings light into darkness. Satan's job is to keep sin hidden so it festers and grows. Thus, putting on this armor brings protection against his schemes.

It might sound a bit ridiculous, but the truth is, you are fighting for your husband and for your marriage when you address the issue of pornography. We are not fighting with literal swords and shields, but this is because we are battling unseen evil forces. Remember, our fight at this moment is not against the porn-makers, but against the devil who tempts us with this fantasy world of escape. We need weapons to equip us as we fight this different kind of battle.

If you read Ephesians 6:10–17, you will find many pieces of armor. All are important, but I want to emphasize the belt of truth. Paul writes in verse 14, "Stand your ground, putting on the belt of truth." The Greek word for "truth" here is *alethia*. It is the exact same word used by Jesus in John 14:6 when He says, "I am the way, the *truth*, and the life" (emphasis mine). Jesus calls himself *alethia*. He is the truth. When we put on the belt of truth, we are in essence putting on Jesus.

I often wish I could go to my closet, pick out Jesus, and wear Him. But since this is not possible, I imagine Him to be right in front of me, asking Him to be a filter for any words that come at me. As I am revealing myself to others and as they respond, Jesus helps me discern which thoughts are useful and edifying. These are the ideas that are allowed passage to my heart. I ask Him to deflect anything that is better fit for another time or place (or not fit for me at all).

Since I am human, there will be things said at different times that I will want to receive but shouldn't. (*"Oh, Jen, don't worry about him using porn! Every guy does it! Save yourself the time and energy! It's an uphill battle. You'll never win."*) And there will be things Jesus wants me to receive but I would rather reject them (*"Jen, you can only begin to rebuild trust by actively trusting again."*) I am not always good at rejecting that which brings me immediate comfort, but with Jesus as my filter, I am better able to discern what will be better for me down the road.

And Jesus always wants what is best for you, friend. He longs for you to partake of His good gifts, which often come by way of community. He never meant for us to do this alone.

CHAPTER 17

Stumbling Blocks for Us All

As iron sharpens iron, so one person sharpens another.

Proverbs 27:17 NIV

Him

It's not easy admitting to someone else that you fail and struggle, especially if that person is someone for whom you care deeply. But that is exactly what I had to do. I had come to the point in my struggles with pornography that I had to share it with others. By this time, Jen knew about it. My parents knew about it as well, but I had so far kept it a secret from the rest of my friends and family.

My mind swirled with questions. *What would people say? How would they respond? Would they treat me any differently? Would they think I was some sort of sexual deviant?*

Was I scared? You bet. Terrified! I imagined all kinds of scenarios of rejection. The whispering behind my back, the judging stares. I could picture myself as the worst form of pariah. But in spite of my fears and trepidations, God kept assuring me. Gently prompting me. Pushing me forward. "This can't stay in the darkness, Craig. It needs to be exposed to My light."

In the past, I had often chided Jen for making a decision without talking to me first because she was concerned about how I would react. She would worry I would respond negatively, and she didn't want to face the conflict that could ensue. However, now I was doing the same thing to everyone I knew. I wasn't giving my friends and family the same courtesy I had been asking from Jen. I was stealing from them the opportunity to show me grace and come alongside me. Conversation has amazing impact on relationships. I was cheating myself out of the help I desperately needed, all because I was scared of the possibility of a negative reaction. But I'm not a coward, am I?

Another reason I didn't want to share my struggles with pornography was because I don't keep it a secret that I'm a Christian. Everyone who knows me knows that I go to church, that I believe in God, and that my faith is important to me. It's interesting that being a Christian somehow gives people the impression that you're a perfect person or at least, you should be pretty close to it. (Maybe we Christians are to blame for that?) As a result, I felt it was necessary to keep my struggles hidden. I needed to keep up appearances. I was afraid to let them see the complete picture of myself, and this showed my lack of trust in the folks who were closest to me. It's amazing how much power we give to fear and shame, and how we let those destructive emotions completely skew our vision of how our friends and family might react.

The first person outside of my family I told about my struggles was the Christian counselor mentioned previously. At first it was awkward and clinical. But it did feel better to talk about it with someone who didn't have an established relationship with me.

The counselor informed me that it was a common problem, which made me feel a little better. He gave me some suggested strategies to help fight the urge to watch pornography. For example, he mentioned that stress is often a trigger for some men, so he suggested exercising regularly as a way to alleviate it. He also mentioned that I should be intimate with my wife as often as possible.

Both of these ideas seemed great. After all, I really needed to exercise more, and what guy doesn't want to be more physically intimate with his wife? However, none of the strategies he provided worked for me long-term. Exercise was something I struggled finding motivation to do at the time. And with two small children who didn't sleep through the night (one of whom slept in our bedroom), increased intimacy with Jen was not always feasible. Eventually I stopped seeing him and I relapsed into my typical behavior.

But that's not to say the counseling was a complete failure. Even though these sessions didn't bring about the "cure" I desired, it accomplished two very important things. First, it gave me practice telling someone my deep, dark secret. Second, it laid groundwork for my recovery by showing me that I really did desire freedom from this affliction.

My counselor told me a story about a man he had previously seen in his practice. He was much older than me, with two grown daughters. The counselor asked this father to tell his college-age daughters about his struggles and ask their forgiveness for being so absent in their lives. The daughters asked hard questions and let their dad see the depth of their anger. They shared the hurt that his addiction caused them, both growing up and presently, now that they were privy to the reason for his absent behavior. But the healing started!

Having two small daughters myself at the time, this story hit home. All I could think was *"I don't want this to be me one day."* It wasn't enough to fully motivate me at the time, but the desire to be free of my sin took firm root.

The Power of a Friend

A little later, Jen and I were discussing my addiction and she began asking me about my friends and if any of them struggled with pornography. I was aware of at least a couple of my friends who actively surfed for and watched porn. Jen asked if I had ever shared with them how much of an issue it was for me.

Of course not.

Hoping this would end the conversation, I told her no. Jen suggested that I discuss it with them and explain my addiction to porn. I was not immediately on board with this, but God worked on my heart and I began to see this as an opportunity for not only me, but for them as well. I wanted to spare them the possible future conversation with *their* grown daughters.

After several days of internal debate and dialogue, I decided to go through with it. I called up my friends and invited them over to hang out. I didn't tell either one of them why I wanted them to come over. I didn't tell them that I wanted to discuss anything serious with them at all. I kept it all close to the vest.

Both of them arrived and after a bit of general conversation I informed them that I wanted to talk to them about something important. The mood of the room became somber. I'm sure they were bracing themselves for some major crisis. And then I just blurted it out. "I'm addicted to porn." I remember that both of them just stared at me for a few moments until one of them spoke, "Wow. I had no idea." Clearly, I had done a good job keeping up appearances.

The rest of our conversation centered on my lifelong struggles with porn. I talked about the times Jen discovered it, the counselor, my cycles of success and failure. I didn't leave anything out. Every now and then, they would ask questions, but for the most part they were silent. At the end of the conversation, I asked for their help. I asked them to pray for me and to help keep me accountable to living porn-free. Both of them agreed, much to my relief!

It's been a couple of years since that conversation and I've shared my struggles with a much wider circle of friends and acquaintances. Jen has talked about our battle on her blog, with her Bible study groups, and at women's conferences. I've shared it with several men who I know are actively fighting the battle against porn. I am amazed at how God has helped us build an incredible support group!

Now my friends know to warn me beforehand about shows or movies that could become stumbling blocks for me. For example, I watched the first couple of seasons of *Game of Thrones*. The storyline is great, but there is quite a bit of explicit sex in the show. I wanted to see season three but was concerned about the amount of sex. I asked a friend to preview the show and let me know if the episodes contained explicit material. As it turns out, my concerns were valid. I didn't watch the show. That's a big win!

Time has proven my initial concerns and fears of rejection as being incorrect. I haven't lost one friend. I haven't had one negative reaction from anyone when I've shared my story. It's been quite the opposite. The most common reaction I get is relief from men and encouragement from women. This should give you a measurable amount of confidence. It's okay to share your story with others.

You may meet resistance or a negative reaction. If so, take a moment to assess why you are receiving it. Pray about it. Ask God to guide you in your conversation. The world is full of broken people, and not everyone knows how to respond. Not everyone will show grace. Usually, negative responses reflect more on them than you. Remember God is sovereign and He wants you to live in freedom. Be honest with yourself and others about who you are and what you've done. God will take care of the rest. Also, don't forget the power of prayer. Ask others to pray for and with you.

Spend time daily reading the Bible. Here are some of my favorite encouraging verses:

- "My dear son, be strong through the grace that God gives you in Christ Jesus" (2 Timothy 2:1).

- "Think about the things of heaven, not the things of earth. For you died to this life, and your real life is hidden with Christ in God. And when Christ, who is your life, is revealed to the whole world, you will share in all his glory" (Colossians 3:2–4).

- "I have told you all this so that you may have peace in me. Here on earth you will have many trials and sorrows. But take heart, because I have overcome the world (John 16:33).

- "I am convinced that nothing can ever separate us from God's love. Neither death nor life, neither angels nor demons, neither our fears for today nor our worries about tomorrow—not even the powers of hell can separate us from God's love. No power in the sky above or in the earth below—indeed, nothing in all creation will ever be able to separate us from the love of God that is revealed in Christ Jesus our Lord" (Romans 8:38–39).

- "I know how to live on almost nothing or with every-thing. I have learned the secret of living in every situation, whether it is with a full stomach or empty, with plenty or little. For I can do everything through Christ, who gives me strength" (Philippians 4:12–13).

My life is different now. I am more aware and cognizant about media that could potentially be dangerous to my recovery. I am willing to work with Jen on setting good boundaries. Just recently, we restarted our cable service. I told her I thought it would be a good idea to put a passcode on the cable box so the temptation to flip to the soft core shows on Cinemax would simply be off-limits. Her doing things like this no longer feels parental to me because I am willing to admit I need help and I greatly desire to limit the number of tempters in my life.

It doesn't have to be an explicit show on TV. Subtle temptations are everywhere, like a Victoria's Secret ad in the mail. This is why filters and passwords can't be my only hope of overcoming porn addiction. To be successful in my battle against temptation, I have to capture each thought as it comes in and think about how my actions can affect others. Mere passwords and filters can't stop all temptations.

Having people in my life who look out for me is vital to my success. We don't live in isolation. We are part of a larger community, the body of Christ. We all struggle to live a godly life, and we all need to reach out and ask for help. We need to be willing to accept this help when it is offered. Our experiences can in turn help others in need. This is one of the reasons we are doing this book. I wanted to use my experiences and struggles to help others. "We know that God causes everything to work together for the good of those who love God and are called according to his purpose for them" (Romans 8:28).

"As iron sharpens iron, so a friend sharpens a friend" (Proverbs 27:17). I first heard this Scripture at a Promise Keepers conference several years ago. It was part of a song being sung by several thousand men in Texas Stadium. It moved me then and it still does today. I believe that we truly are our brother's keeper. Men need to pull together in this war and fight together. In the war against pornography, there is no such thing as an army of one.

Call to Action

You may not be there yet, but soon you're going to have to tell someone about your addiction and struggles with pornography. If you haven't already, the first person should be your wife. That's not going to be easy, but it's a necessary step in your recovery. Pornography has driven a wedge between you and your spouse. It's time to remove it and restore the relationship to the condition God has ordained. When you were married, you became one flesh. Don't allow pornography to separate you.

Next, find someone who is trustworthy and who can and will pray for and with you. I find it helpful to let this person know they can ask you hard questions and hold you accountable to be honest with your answers. To be frank, this can prove to be really difficult, especially for those of us who are afraid to admit failure. I have to think about what I truly want to get out of these conversations: am I seeking the approval of my friend or am I seeking freedom? Covering things up and leaving them in darkness are not moving me closer to recovery, but actually set me back significantly because I'm refusing to let light touch my sin. If Jesus is calling you to use this tool as part of your journey to recovery, He will help you find this person. The Holy Spirit will help you to choose confession over your pride. I have found that the relationships God has brought into my life are a powerful weapon in my fight against porn. Not only do they help me turn away from porn, but they also help point me on a path that leads to a deeper relationships with Jesus.

Finally, and this is a hard one, you need to allow your wife to talk about it with others. At the beginning, before Jen would share our story, she would tell me who she would be sharing it with and why. She was allowing me to say no. I never did. By giving me the background, it provided me with context and helped keep me from feeling exposed.

This fight is going to be a daily decision that you make. Each day will bring its own new set of challenges and joys. Be thankful for them. Always remember this: God loves you just as you are and He will never abandon you. He will sustain you and carry you through. Often this support will come from people who love you and want to see you succeed. Lean on Him and them at all times. Seek time with God daily. He's cheering you on and so am I.

CHAPTER 18

Remember Delight

Place me like a seal over your heart,
like a seal on your arm.
For love is as strong as death,
its jealousy as enduring as the grave.
Love flashes like fire,
the brightest kind of flame.
Many waters cannot quench love,
nor can rivers drown it.
If a man tried to buy love
with all his wealth,
his offer would be utterly scorned.

Song of Solomon 8:6–7

I knew the moment he picked up his guitar and opened his mouth to lead worship in front of a rowdy bunch of junior high kids that I loved him. He would be my husband. I was barely twenty and we had been dating all of maybe six days, but this unmistakable stirring in my heart was love. I had never experienced *this* love before. Though I may have been young and naïve and people doubted that I could *know* so early in the game, I did know. This was what I had been waiting for all my short life.

I always wanted to marry early. I wanted to be someone's only. I wanted to love fiercely and exclusively. I wanted to be loved and protected. And God built these desires into me. He designed me to be tenacious and loyal and to rise up if someone or something tries to take what He has meant for me to have.

We are made in the image of our God, and as such, our hearts are created to beat much like His. Just as I am jealous for my husband, God is jealous for us. It's not a worldly form of jealousy. It's not the kind played out on shows like *Desperate Housewives* or *The Bachelor*. If you look at the Hebrew word used for "jealousy," it is *qinah*, which means zeal. It's a fervor, an intense, warm feeling of devotion. It's not about winning a competition or keeping a worldly prize, but about a kind of passion God created you to have for your spouse. This passion you feel is just a small portion of the same kind of passion God feels for you.

I don't know about you, but Craig and I have both experienced times where we forget about how passionate God is about us. We forget His immeasurable love and the fact that He delights in us, despite our propensity to sin.

Just yesterday in my quiet time, I turned to a clean page in my journal and there, typed in pretty blue ink were these simple words: *"God delights in you."* I started to smile and then stopped myself. All I could think of was *"but . . ."*

But, I yelled at my kids yesterday.
I probably should have helped my friend more.
I didn't pray as much as I should have.
I spent too much money.

I could have continued with all my *"buts,"* but God interjected. *"There are no buts. I delight in you. Period."* He will not always be delighted by my actions, as I continually fall short of His glory, but He is delighted by my pursuit of Him, when I confess to Him, when I praise Him. My delighting in Him, leaning on Him, seeking Him brings Him great joy. Zephaniah writes:

> For the LORD your God is living among you.
> He is a mighty savior.
> He will take *delight* in you with gladness.
> With his love, he will calm all your fears.
> He will rejoice over you with joyful songs.
>   (3:17, emphasis mine)

God delights in me even though He knows I will not always choose to act the way He desires me to act. He sees me "becoming in practice what we are positionally in Christ."[1] His delight is not based on my ability to perform perfectly (thank goodness because it will never happen), but on how He sees me through Christ—redeemed. Will He still discipline me? Yes. Will He continue to teach me to better reflect His love? Yes. Will He continue to pursue me despite my imperfections? Yes.

Why does He do this? Because He is fierce about love. Because He IS love. Because His love cannot be quenched by any amount of sin and nothing is strong enough to sweep it away. And if God loves me this way, I want to be able to love Craig this way. Craig wants to be able to love me this way. We desire for our love to be a blazing fire and worth more than all wealth.

How do wives love like this when porn is a problem? How do husbands love when they feel like they are being manhandled and controlled by their wives? How do we desire and touch each other when it feels like there is a thick stone wall between us, comprised of fear, rejection, insecurity, mistrust, doubt, and anger? How do we take delight when all we can see is grime, the filth of each other's sins?

We remember.

Remember Past Delights

Something powerful happens when we return to moments in our past that have deeply impacted us. Activating these memories stir feelings, even ones that have lay dormant for quite some time. When I relive the moment of seeing Craig leading worship for the first time, I see all the good I saw in him that night. My body is jolted by those feelings of new attraction and the unadulterated hope I had for our future. I remember why I fell in love. And I remember that God brought us together for a reason and purpose He saw was good.

Continually throughout the Old Testament, God tells the Israelites to remember, too. In 1 Chronicles 16, King David delivers this psalm, possibly the first one ever used in a tabernacle service:

> *Remember* the wonders he has performed,
> his miracles, and the rulings he has given,
> you children of his servant Israel,
> you descendants of Jacob, his chosen ones.
> He is the LORD our God.
> His justice is seen throughout the land.
> *Remember* his covenant forever—
> the commitment he made to a thousand generations.
>   (vv. 12–15, emphasis mine)

Twice David reminds his people to remember all God has done and the promises He has made to them. Throughout the entire song, David implores the Israelites to give thanks for what God has done in their lives—for His provision, their deliverance, and the strength He has given them to endure treacherous trials. He knows that their remembrance and gratitude will fortify their souls, creating an oasis when they feel spiritually or physically dry and weak.

Just as the Israelites could recall the fiery pillars that led them through the wilderness after their escape from Egypt and the manna that dropped from the sky to fill their hungry stomachs, I can remember times Craig loved me and loved me well. I sit and think about how he cried with me when I discovered my hearing loss was more severe than I thought and I would have to wear hearing aids in order to do my job as a special education teacher well. I think about the time he got the sewing machine off the high shelf and helped his youngest daughter sew a dress for her stuffed rabbit. I think about the coupon books he made me our first Christmases after I starting staying home with the girls because we couldn't afford to buy presents for each other.

All of those times, I delighted in my husband. To remember those events from the past elicits that same feeling of delight I had when the events originally occurred. I am refilled with pleasure and enjoyment. I become enraptured by moments profoundly good. Remembering helps to shift my perspective. Instead of seeing my husband as a person who has hurt me with his addiction, I see a more complete picture of him. Yes, he has sinned, but he is so much more than that sin. And if I spend enough time remembering the good, the sin pales in comparison with who God created him to be for me as a husband.

These memories also help me to delight in him in the present, too, which allows me to love him better. As I am reminded of the good times, I seek to look for those glimmers of goodness in the present moment, no matter how dark that moment may be.

Even from a scientific point of view there is value in this process of remembering. Recently, a New York University research team discovered that one act of remembering can influence your future acts.[2] Essentially, the study measured subjects' responses to objects in three categories: novel objects, repeated objects (exactly the same as the original object), and objects that are *similar to* the initial stimulus. Researchers presented the subject with an initial novel object. If the next stimulus following the novel object was exactly the same as the initial picture, the subjects were more *likely to label all subsequent objects presented as the same as the initial object*, even if some of those presented later were actually slightly different. However, if researchers presented the novel object and then, immediately following, presented an object that was only similar, the subject was more likely to see the subtle shift in details and label the images presented after these two correctly as either "similar" or "old."

How can we extrapolate this out to apply to our memories and our marriages? Obviously, we don't live in scientifically controlled environments and we don't have researchers who point out subtle shifts in our spouse's behaviors. What we do have is evidence that noticing new things increases the likelihood that we will continue on the path of noticing even more new things. When we remember delightful times or events and take time to notice new similar times and events, we become more apt to steadily recognize the good aspects of our spouse and our marriage. Make it a point to pull a good memory out about your spouse every day and watch for things he or she does that bring you delight, on a small scale or a large scale. Then, share your delight with your spouse with words of praise and thanksgiving. Thank God for those moments, too.

Remember the Bigger Picture

When Craig remembers events from our past, it's not so much to elicit the specific feelings of delight, but to keep the big picture in the forefront of his mind. Thoughts of our first dance as a married couple filter into his mind. Why this? Perhaps because of the words of the song. B.B. King's "Since I Met You Baby" talks about how his whole life has changed since he met his woman and how happy he now is. Reliving that dance allows Craig to see how much good has come into his life since we've met and the momentary trial seems to lessen a bit in its importance.

Time and time again, God sent prophets during the Old Testament times to remind His people that their current trial was not a state of permanence. The Israelites spent years in captivity in Babylon, unable to live their lives with the freedom to worship their God without punishment. Their entire way of life changed and many of them longed to return to their land, their ways, and their God. In Isaiah, God reminds His people that their captivity is temporary and He will send rescue:

> But I carry out the predictions of my prophets!
> By them I say to Jerusalem, "People will live here again,"
> and to the towns of Judah, "You will be rebuilt;
> I will restore all your ruins!"
> When I speak to the rivers and say, "Dry up!"
> they will be dry.
> When I say of Cyrus, "He is my shepherd,"
> he will certainly do as I say.
> He will command, "Rebuild Jerusalem";
> he will say, "Restore the Temple." (44:26–28)

God will lead you out of captivity, friends. He promises not to leave us in the wilderness. Just as He led the Israelites out of the wilderness into the Promised Land and just has He restored the temple after Cyrus released them back to Jerusalem, God will restore your marriage from the tarnishing effects of porn addiction as you surrender it to Him. Restoration is the big picture here. A unity like you have never experienced is possible. All you may see right now is ruins. But God does beautiful repairs to broken things. How do we know? Because we live it.

Craig and I don't have a perfect marriage now. One of my friends asked me recently if we were a "10" on the marriage scale. I believe she meant, is everything roses since we've gone through this journey of recovery? I don't know how to measure marriage on that kind of scale, but if I could quantify anything, I'd say we've increased the amount of grace we give each other. Perhaps because we remember we're human. We remember the good. We remember how far God has brought us and it gives us hope for what is to come.

For you to do together:

1. Spend some time discussing both pivotal and mundane moments in your dating and marriage history that brought you great joy and delight. Write a few of these down and keep them in a place where you might see them often. This will encourage you to remember.

2. Read Joshua 4 together. Then, think of the last few weeks. What good things has your spouse done for you (big or little) that brought you joy, delight, and gratitude? Get some smooth stones, a large, pretty container, and write one word on each stone that describes these things. As you continue on in your marriage journey, add a stone when another good thing transpires in your marriage. This is an

altar of remembrance you are building in thanksgiving to God for the good things in your marriage.

3. Make a list of fun things you'd both like to do together. Revisit places where your relationship started (if possible). Design an adventure to create new memories. Make date nights a priority and realize they don't have to cost a lot of money. Date nights are just about being together.

4. Hold hands. Bow your heads in prayer. Say a few sentences to God, giving thanks for specific aspects of your marriage.

Resources

Books for marital growth

Chapman, Gary. *The Five Love Languages: The Secret to Love That Lasts*. Chicago: Northfield Publishing, 1995.

Eggerichs, Emerson. *Love and Respect: The Love She Most Desires; The Respect He Desperately Needs*. Nashville: Thomas Nelson, 2004.

Renfroe, John and Anita. *Songs in the Key of Solomon: In the Word and in the Mood*. Colorado Springs, CO: David C. Cook, 2007.

Yerkovich, Milan and Kay. *How We Love*. Colorado Springs, CO: WaterBrook Press, 2006.

Books to help men with porn addiction

Arterburn, Stephen, Fred Stoker, and Mike Yorkey. *Every Man's Battle: Every Man's Guide to Winning the War on Sexual Temptation One Victory at a Time*. Colorado Springs, CO: WaterBrook Press, 2000.

Arterburn, Stephen, Fred Stoker, and Mike Yorkey. *Every Man's Battle Guide: Weapons for the War Against Sexual Temptation*. Colorado Springs, CO: WaterBrook Press, 2009.

Arterburn, Stephen, Fred Stoker, and Mike Yorkey. *Every Man's Battle Workbook: The Path to Sexual Integrity Starts Here.* Colorado Springs, CO: WaterBrook Press, 2002.

Books for women regarding self-image/insecurity

Cherry, Lynn Marie. *Keep Walking.* Available at www.lynn mariecherry.com.

Moore, Beth. *So Long Insecurity: You've Been a Bad Friend to Us.* Carol Stream, IL: Tyndale, 2010.

Eldredge, John and Stasi. *Captivating: Unveiling the Mystery of a Woman's Soul.* Nashville: Thomas Nelson, 2007.

Books for spiritual growth

Gross, Craig, and Jason Harper. *Jesus Loves You, This I Know.* Grand Rapids: Baker, 2009.

Lucado, Max. *Facing Your Giants.* Nashville: Thomas Nelson, 2008.

Moore, Beth. *Praying God's Word: Breaking Free from Spiritual Strongholds.* Nashville: B&H, 2009.

Swindoll, Charles. *David: A Man of Passion and Destiny.* Nashville: Thomas Nelson, 2000.

Daily Devotionals

Chambers, Oswald. *My Utmost for His Highest.* Grand Rapids, Discovery House Publishers, 1992. See also utmost.org.

Dungy, Tony, and Nathan Whitaker. *The One-Year Uncommon Life Daily Challenge.* Carol Stream, IL: Tyndale, 2011.

The High Calling Daily Reflections. http://www.thehighcalling .org/reflections.

Swenson, Richard. *A Minute of Margin: Restoring Balance to Busy Lives—180 Daily Reflections*. Colorado Springs, CO: NavPress, 2003.

Young, Sarah. *Jesus Calling: Enjoying Peace in His Presence*. Nashville: Thomas Nelson, 2004.

For Men

Briscoe, Stuart. *The One-Year Devotions for Men*. Carol Stream, IL: Tyndale, 2001.

The Drive-Time Message for Men 1: Daily Devotions for Your Commute. Colorado Springs, CO: NavPress, 2006. Audiobook, 1 CD.

Eldredge, John. *Wild at Heart: Discovering the Secret of a Man's Soul*. Nashville: Thomas Nelson, 2001.

Finding a counselor

Mitch Temple. "Selecting a Christian Counselor." Focus on the Family. http://www.focusonthefamily.com/marriage/divorce_and_infidelity/when_your_marriage_needs_help/finding_a_christian_counselor.aspx.

"Finding a Christian Counselor." FamilyLife. http://www.familylife.com/articles/topics/marriage/troubled-marriage/counseling-issues/finding-a-christian-counselor#.U6MFUbRnA2s.

American Association of Christian Counselors: http://www.aacc.net/resources/find-a-counselor/.

If you are being abused

The National Domestic Violence Hotline, 1–800–799–7233 or www.thehotline.org.

Prayers

Prayer is crucial to your individual spiritual growth and to your marriage. Below we have included some prayers you can pray daily for yourselves and for each other. We've also included a prayer of confession and a declaration of forgiveness that reminds us of the sin-cleansing power of Jesus' death and resurrection.

For a wife to pray over her husband

Lord, I pray my husband would be strong in you and in your mighty power. May he remember, every day, to put on the armor you so willingly supply to us so he may stand firm against all strategies the devil employs. May he put on the belt of truth and the breastplate of your righteousness. May his feet be fitted with the shoes of peace. May he forever hold in his hand the shield of faith that will deflect the arrows the enemy throws against him. On his head may he wear the helmet of salvation. In his hands, may he carry the sword of the Spirit—the very Word of God. May he always know that you are with him, that you hear his prayers, and that you desire to walk with him every day of his life. Amen.

Based on Ephesians 6:10–18.

For a husband to pray over his wife

Lord, I pray that my wife knows that you knit her together in her mother's womb, perfectly and completely. I pray she would know that she doesn't have to conform to worldly patterns in order to be acceptable and loved by me. I pray she would grow in her trust of you, and you would teach her how to forgive me and trust me again. Together, may we fix our eyes on whatever is true, honorable, right, pure, lovely, and admirable. Amen.

Based on Psalm 139:13; Matthew 18:22–24; Romans 12:2; Philippians 4:8.

For a wife to pray for herself

My faithful God, help me to call this to mind and therefore always have hope: Because of Your great love, I am not consumed, for Your compassions never fail. They are new toward me every morning; great is Your faithfulness. I will say to myself, "The Lord is my portion; therefore I will wait for Him." Amen.

Based on Lamentations 3:22–24. Taken from Beth Moore, Praying God's Word *(Nashville: B&H, 2009).*

For a husband to pray for himself

Lord, I renounce all these uses of my body as an instrument of unrighteousness and by so doing ask You to break all bondages that Satan has brought into my life through that involvement. I confess my participation. I now present my body to You as a living sacrifice, holy and acceptable to You, and I reserve the sexual use of my body only for marriage. I renounce the lie of Satan that my body is not clean, that it is dirty or in any way unacceptable as a result of my past sexual experiences. Lord, I thank You that You have totally cleansed and forgiven me, that You love and accept me unconditionally. Therefore, I can accept myself. And I choose to do so, to accept myself and my body as cleansed. In Jesus' name. Amen.

Based on Genesis 2:24; Romans 12:1–2; Hebrews 13:4. Taken from Neil Anderson, The Bondage Breaker *(Eugene, OR: Harvest House, 1990).*

Prayer of confession

I confess to Almighty God . . . that I have sinned by my own fault in thought, word, and deed, in things done and left undone; especially _____. For these and all other sins which I cannot now remember, I am truly sorry. I pray God to have mercy on me. I firmly intend amendment of life, and I humbly beg forgiveness . . .

Taken from The Book of Common Prayer.

Declaration of forgiveness

Our Lord Jesus Christ, who offered himself to be sacrificed for us to the Father, forgives your sins by the grace of the Holy Spirit. Amen.

Taken from The Book of Common Prayer.

Notes

Introduction

1 Rebecca Grace, "When Dad Falls: A Family's Ordeal with Pornography," *Crosswalk*, September 9, 2004. http://www.crosswalk.com/family/parenting/when-dad-falls-a-familys-ordeal-with-pornography-1284103.html.

2 Mark A. Yarhouse, "Marriage Related Research," *Christian Counseling Today* 12, no. 1 (2004).

3 Jason S. Carroll, Laura M. Padilla-Walker, Larry J. Nelson, Chad D. Olson, Carolyn McNamara Barry, Stephanie D. Madsen, "Generation XXX: Pornography Acceptance and Use Among Emerging Adults," *Journal of Adolescent Research*, Volume 23, Number 1 (January 2008): 6–30.

4 Archibald D. Hart, *The Sexual Man* (Dallas: Word, 1994).

5 "Evangelicals Are Addicted To Porn," *ChristiaNet.com*, http://christiannews.christianet.com/1154951956.htm.

Chapter 2

1 Cisterns are waterproof containers typically used for catching and storing rainwater, usually in arid areas.

2 Derek Abma, "Men Think of Sex Only 19 Times a Day, Report Finds," *The Vancouver Sun*, November 30, 2011.

Chapter 3

1 Ryan Singel, "Internet Porn: Worse Than Crack?" *Wired.com*, November 19, 2004, http://www.wired.com/science/discoveries/news/2004/11/65772.

2 Christian Grove, Brian Joseph Gillespie, Tracy Royce, and Janet Lever, "Perceived Consequences of Casual Online Sexual Activities on Heterosexual Relationships: A U.S. Online Survey," *Archives of Sexual Behavior* 40, no. 2 (February 20, 2010): 429–39.

3 Amanda M. Maddox, Galena K. Rhoades, and Howard J. Markman, "Viewing Sexually-explicit Materials Alone or Together: Associations with Relationship Quality," *Archives of Sexual Behavior* 40, no. 2 (December 29, 2009): 441–48.

4 Ross Douthat, "Is Pornography Adultery?" *The Atlantic*, October 2008, http://www.theatlantic.com/.

5 In this passage, Jesus quotes from Genesis 1:27 and Genesis 5:2, and then Genesis 2:24.

6 2 Corinthians 12:9.

7 Philippians 4:19.

8 Matthew 19:6.

Chapter 4

1 Jenna Sauers, "The Unretouched Photos That Victoria's Secret Doesn't Want You to See," *Jezebel*, October 17, 2012, http://jezebel.com/.

2 Shelley Lubben, "Porn Industry," www.shelleylubben.com/porn-industry.

3 Bryce Wagoner, *After Porn Ends*, Marina del Rey: Oxymoron Entertainment, 2010.

4   This quote was in response to a question posed in the documentary *After Porn Ends*, in why she continued in the porn business despite knowing that this was not what she really wanted to do with her life. Crissy has since gotten out of the porn business, given her life to Christ, and speaks about God's redemption.

Chapter 5

1   Mark 4:3–20.

Chapter 6

1   Skip Moen, "Leverage," Hebrew Word Study, February 18, 2010, http://skipmoen.com/.
2   Matt Carter, "The Gospel and Sex," January 27, 2013, http://austinstone.org/sermons/item/sex.
3   "Blue Letter Bible," www.blueletterbible.org.
4   1 John 4:16.

Chapter 7

1   Genesis 50:20, Romans 8:28.
2   Stormie Omartian, *The Power of a Praying Wife* (Eugene, OR: Harvest House, 1997).

Chapter 8

1   Matthew 7:3–5.
2   Genesis 2:18.
3   Emerson Eggerichs, *Love and Respect: The Love She Most Desires, the Respect He Desperately Needs* (Nashville, TN: Integrity Publishers, 2004), 56.

Chapter 9

1   Dictionary.com, http://dictionary.reference.com/.

2   M. H. Manser, *Dictionary of Bible Themes: The Accessible and Comprehensive Tool for Topical Studies* (London: Martin Manser, 2009).

3   R. Jamieson, A. R. Fausset, and D. Brown, "Hebrews 6:18," *Commentary Critical and Explanatory on the Whole Bible* (Oak Harbor, WA: Logos Research Systems, Inc., 1997).

Chapter 10

1   "The Twelve Steps of Alcoholics Anonymous," www.aa.org.

2   "Repent," Dictionary.com, http://dictionary.reference.com/.

Chapter 11

1   John MacArthur, *Alone with God* (Wheaton, IL: Victor Books, 1995).

2   Lit. *Non nobis domine sed nomini tuo da gloriam.*

3   Kevin Skinner, "Is Porn Really Destroying 500,000 Marriages Annually?" *Psychology Today*, December 12, 2011, http://www.psychologytoday.com/blog/inside-porn-addiction/201112/is-porn-really-destroying-500000-marriages-annually.

4   We're referring to the Kubler-Ross model of grief. There are five stages: denial, anger, bargaining, depression, and acceptance.

Chapter 12

1   Roman law had removed the Jews' right to use capital punishment.

2   See Leviticus 20:10 and Deuteronomy 22:22.

3   1 John 1:5.

4   W. Hall Harris, Michael W. Holmes, and Rick Brannan, *The Lexham English Bible English-Greek Reverse Interlinear New Testament* (Bellingham, WA: Logos Bible Software, 2010).

Chapter 13

1   Ephesians 6:10–19 (additional explanation of the armor of God in chapter 16).
2   Genesis 2:18.

Chapter 15

1   Beth Moore, *So Long, Insecurity: You've Been a Bad Friend to Us* (Carol Stream, IL: Tyndale House, 2010), xiii.
2   http://www.heraldmag.org/olb/contents/dictionaries/SHebrew.pdf. Retrieved June 4, 2013.
3   John 6:22–66.
4   Matthew 26:69–75.
5   John 21:15–17.
6   Romans 8:31.
7   John 7:38.

Chapter 16

1   Jennie Allen, *Chase* (Nashville: Thomas Nelson, 2012), 34.

Chapter 18

1   John Piper, "Why God Tells Us He Delights in His Children," *Desiring God*, August 23, 2006, http://www.desiringgod.org/articles/why-god-tells-us-he-delights-in-his-children.

2   Lila Davachi and Arhanti Sadanand, "One Act of Remembering Can Influence Future Acts," NYU.edu, July 26, 2012, http:
//www.nyu.edu/about/news-publications/news/2012/07/26
/one-act-of-remembering-can-influence-future-acts
-nyu-researchers-find-.html.

Acknowledgments

First, thank you, Jesus, for giving us the words in this book. They would not have come out in this way without your power, love, and grace. And thank you for being a God who wastes nothing, who acknowledges every tear and heartache, who turns into good what Satan meant for harm. Thank you for being the very breath of our healing.

Second, thank you to the amazing team at Discovery House, for being a family, for having faith in us, and for being such amazing disciples of Christ. Miranda and Tim, I really don't have enough space or know enough adjectives to fully describe how much your partnership has meant to us.

Next, thank you, Jody Collins, for doing the first run of edits for us. Thank you for being the person to step up and tell us when our words weren't making sense. But thank you, also, for your prayers and encouragement. It has been a joy to have you be a part of this process.

Thank you to our prayer support network, the people to whom I could fire off a prayer request at a moment's notice and know y'all were taking it to Jesus on our behalf: Nancy & Kevin, Mari & Dan, Jenny & Justin, Travis & Catherine, Cindy, Nancy, Kimberly, Paul & Lexi, and Paula & Bill. Thank you also to my girls, The Soli Deo Gloria Sisterhood, who have prayed us through this process without ceasing. Y'all were there for me when I started telling this story.

And to all our friends and family for holding us up, for cheering us on, for responding to impromptu (and sometimes frantic) Facebook requests for information and ideas, thank you from the core of our being. There are so many people who span the globe who have virtually held us, but whom we may have never physically touched. But if we could put your face in our hands and speak to you, this is what we would say:

Dear You,

God has used you. Thank you so much for letting Him, for in this process, you have deeply touched our hearts and perhaps the very people who right now hold this book in their hands. You have prayed. You have listened. You have allowed us to be privy to your stories, your ideas, and your time. You have given us a piece of yourself and let me tell you, it is treasured.

Your encouragement has gotten us through some dark nights of our souls. Revisiting this pain, staying focused in the present, and not fearing the future were only made possible because of the words God gave you to keep us afloat. When we doubted, you reminded us of our faith, our mission, and our heart for those who are in a desperate kind of pain of which we happen to know.

I (Jen) would like to thank the bloggers who allowed me to share my story on their personal corners of the Internet, the ones who got me writing about this in the first place. Thank you for creating safe communities for authenticity to blossom and grow and touch others.

We both are incredibly indebted to our prayer supporters who agreed to pray every time we sent out an e-mail pleading for help. And thank you to Jody, who saved us much time

Acknowledgments

rewriting because she so lovingly edited and helped us make sure our ideas were clear.

Soli Deo Gloria,
Craig and Jen

Note to the Reader

The publisher invites you to share your response to the message of this book by writing Discovery House Publishers, P.O. Box 3566, Grand Rapids, MI 49501, U.S.A. For information about other Discovery House books, music, or DVDs, contact us at the same address or call 1-800-653-8333. Find us on the Internet at dhp.org or send e-mail to books@dhp.org.

About the Authors

Craig and Jen have been married since 2000. They love spending their time with their lovely daughters and two (rather high maintenance) dogs in Austin, Texas.

You can connect with Jen at her blog for women and on Facebook:

- www.solideogloriasisterhood.com

- www.facebook.com/solideogloriasisterhood